THE
MACARONI'S
IN THE
BASEMENT

THE
MACARONI'S
IN THE
BASEMENT

FRAN CLARO

CHANGING LIVES PRESS

Changing Lives Press

WWW.CHANGINGLIVESPRESS.COM

TO PURCHASE OUR BOOKS, PLEASE VISIT OUR WEBSITE AT
WWW.CONTINENTALSALESINC.COM
OR CONTACT TERRY WYBEL, CONTINENTAL SALES, INC.,
AT WYBELT@WYBEL.COM OR CALL 1-847-381-6530.

OUR TITLES ARE FOCUSED ON BOOKS THAT IMPACT LIVES.
THE AUTHORS WE CHOOSE ARE THOSE WHO HAVE INFLUENCED OR
CHANGED THE WAY WE THINK, ACT, OR PROCESS IDEAS AND INFORMATION.

DESIGN: NOËL CLARO
PHOTOGRAPHY: NATASHA CLARO SOUTHWICK
COVER ILLUSTRATION: IAIN BURKE

PRINTED IN THE UNITED STATES OF AMERICA

10 9 8 7 6 5 4 3 2 1

CONTENTS

Meet the Nonnas   1

Spring

Hurry Up . . . The Bride's Getting Out of the Car: **Sausage and Peppers** and **Bread Salad**   10

Toss Me a Salami: The Football Wedding: **Olive Salad**   14

A Dinner Party: **Eggplant Parmigiana**   18

In the Style of the Shoemaker: **Chicken Scarpariello**   22

Price Wars: **Escarole with Beans and "Bacon"**   25

A Semi-Private Bath: **Friday Night Fish Soup**   28

Across the Alley: **Pork Chops with Wine and Sage**   31

Palm Sunday: **Pizza Rustica**   34

A Barley vs. Grain Spat: **Easter Grain Pie**   39

New Spot for a Garden: **Crostata Marmellata or Jam Tart**   43

A Live Show: **Roast Chicken**   46

Saturday at the Movies: **Steak Pizzaiola**   49

The Saint's Big Day: **Porchetta or Pork Roast**   52

It's All in a Name: **Stuffato or Pot Roast**   55

Getting Sauced: **"Instant" Gravy and Meatballs**   58

Summer

Waw-de-mell-OWN, Tutti Frutti and the Ladies from the Block: **Watermelon Granita**   63

Fire Hydrant Days: **Chicken Milanese and Salad**   67

Sand in Their Shoes: **Potato Frittata** 70

Fireworks: **Veal Parmigiana** 73

How the Garden Grows: **Stuffed Zucchini** 76

The War of the Flowers: **Stuffed Zucchini Blossoms** and **Zucchini Blossom Frittata** 79

The Name Game: **Romano Beans in Sauce** and **Romano Beans with Ham** 82

A Block Party: **Cream Puffs** 85

Guarding the Fireside: **Baked Pork and Beans** 89

My Town's Better Than Your Town: **Caponata or Eggplant Relish** 92

Hot Stuff: **Slow-Fried Hot Peppers** 95

We Need the Eggs: **Western Omelet** 98

A Winery—in Brooklyn?: **Peaches in Red Wine** and **Pears Simmered in Red Wine** 100

Preserving the Past: **Coconut Jelly Layer Cake** 103

Covering a Fig Tree: **Fig Pizza** 106

Fall

Problems! Problems!: **Pasta with Peas and Pancetta** 110

TV Time: **Popcorn** and **Taralli** 113

The Macaroni's in the Basement: **Macaroni and Gravy** 117

The World at Their Doorstep: **Onions and Eggs** 121

The Statue's Eyes Moved: **Venetian Friday Fish** 124

Photographic Memories: **Lasagna Genovese** 126

Piecework: **Spiedini** 129

Homework: **Eggs in Purgatory** 132

Sewing for Fun: **Regina Cookies** 135

Church Ladies: **Ribollita** 138

A Storefront Caravan: **Beef Paprikash** 142

Anything for Thanksgiving?: **Stuffed Mushrooms** 146

Winter

Let the Season Start: **Angeletti or Lemon–Iced Cookies**   150

Celebrating a Saint: **Biscotti**   154

Ready for a Wedding: **Wedding Soup**   157

Nonnas and the Red Menace: **Pasta with Anchovies**   161

Queen of the Transfers: **Codfish in Tomato Sauce**   164

The Christmas Eve Feast: **Sicilian Pasta with Sardines, Neapolitan Pasta,**   167
   Neapolitan Baccala, Sicilian Baccala, Fritto Misto (Fried Fish), Neapolitan Fish
   Salad, Sicilian Mussels, Neapolitan Baked Red Snapper, Livornese Pasta with
   Clam Sauce, Calabrese Calamari, Sicilian Escarole Pie, Neapolitan Spinach Pie

A Baby Is Born: **Baccala Montecato**   179

Happy New Year: **Zeppole**   182

For Mary, my mom.
Solo per te le mia canzone vola

Meet the Nonnas

Meet Maddelana, Giuseppina, Concetta, and Aniella,
the shortest, liveliest grandmas in their Brooklyn neighborhood. They are
exhaling a post-War sigh of relief—dancing at block parties, celebrating
births and weddings, and marveling at the Coney Island fireworks on
Tuesday nights. They share an attitude of seeming nonchalance while
working night and day, and a love for anything related to family, faith, and
food. It's their cooking that they are passionate about. Their language is
food; their currency is recipes.

Maddelana is a grandmother of seven. She is a cousin to Concetta and a
sister to Giuseppina. She and Concetta live on the same block in different
tenements. Bedecked with a necklace of rosary beads, she has boundless
energy and always nibbles on whatever she finds in a neighbor's house.
Maddelana is extremely religious—she makes novenas, cleans churches,
and irons priests' vestments. Her mother is still alive at the age of 90. Her
husband was shell-shocked after being mustard-gassed in World War I.
Maddelana is so-o-o-o thrifty—she's the queen of the transit transfers and
can travel from one end of Brooklyn to the other on a five-cent trolley ride.

Giuseppina is a grandmother of two, a sister to Maddelana, and a
cousin to Concetta. She considers herself a lady of the manor and insists
on drinking tea out of a glass while her cronies sip their coffee from cups.
Her major hobby is smoking Chesterfields. She works as a seamstress
and even sews as a hobby. But her major role in life is to play sick. Her
daughters tolerate her. She is a gossip who lives in a two-family house
on a nicer block than the others do in their tenements. She has diamond
rings that gleam in the sun. Giuseppina leaves visits to her 90-year-old
mother up to her sister, Maddelana.

Concetta, a grandmother of 12, is an immigrant from Naples, like her cousins. She works as a seamstress and takes in whatever homework she can find. Her hobby is housekeeping—eat off her floor if you will. She fears her daughters might move to the suburbs. She is a superb cook of the old school—Christmas and Easter pastries, soups, stews, pastas. She often mentions the one son who "goes to business" in Manhattan. Other sons and sons-in-law are city workers, trolley drivers, sanitation men. Her daughters work with her in a neighborhood sewing shop. She dotes on her grandchildren but has some trouble relating to her Irish daughters-in-law. She stands up for herself by wearing a necklace given to her by a former suitor at her marriage to Calogero.

Aniella, a grandmother of eight, is the outsider because she is an immigrant from (drum roll, please) Sicily. She works along with her daughter as a seamstress and lives in an apartment in the same tenement as Concetta. She challenges her Neapolitan neighbors over recipes. When she can afford it, she takes a summer bungalow with her family near one that Concetta rents with her family. She casually drops a dollar bill in the church collection basket—always making sure that her neighbors witness the act. She is a softie with her grandchildren.

Calogero, Concetta's husband, is a construction worker. He won her heart when a friend, Concetta's cousin, introduced him to her. He adores his grandchildren, helps with holiday baking, and organizes and collects money for an annual saint's feast day.

I love the quartet, the women, who meet on their way to church and talk about what they made for dinner. Giuseppina is always shaking her head in disapproval, thinking her fish was tastier than the soup her companion served. Concetta sticks two fingers down the collars of her grandchildren's coats to find out if they are cold. Maddelana throws coins wrapped in a handkerchief from a second-story window for the grandchildren to buy ice cream. Aniella allows the grandchildren to rifle her photo albums and discover relatives from a faraway place.

I love the nonnas, who make caustic remarks about one another's cooking, share recipes with a mine-is-better-than-yours certainty, and argue about the benefits of scrubbing or peeling a zucchini. I love them for fixing dishes that were sublime. My original intent was to capture their kitchen magic in a cookbook. Then I realized recipes alone can't adequately convey their spirit, nor the spirit of the time when their lives were centered on a five-block radius, including the church, the stores, the school. So their everyday lives—their interaction with one another, their concern for their grandchildren, their slightly suspicious nature, their raised eyebrows while accepting a son's Irish fiancée—have become the fabric of the tales that accompany their recipes.

Their families are close. No one lives more than three blocks from even distant relatives. In one or the other's kitchen, Maddelana, Concetta, and Aniella meet to sip coffee and hint at what they might be cooking for dinner. On a regular basis, Giuseppina stops by to have a glass of hot tea and to criticize her sister, Maddelana. In her presence, the others wave their arms wildly to rid their kitchens of smoke from her ever-present cigarette.

They have managed to get their families through the Depression, to keep their children safe from crippling polio. They work—and bicker—with their daughters and daughters-in-law in neighborhood sewing factories that materialize like pop-up shops. And they skillfully handle household funds—all without a GED.

Ever resourceful, they serve food on plates they got when local theaters featured Dish Night during the Depression. They each took home a free soup bowl for the price of a movie ticket. As eager as they are to show their individuality, they overlook the fact that every china closet on the Avenue is filled with identical tureens, coffee cups, and platters, courtesy of Fred Astaire films.

IN THE KITCHEN WITH THE NONNAS

The kitchen belongs to the nonnas. On Sunday mornings, Concetta allows her husband, Calogero, to approach a simmering pot of gravy. His job is to dip a crust of bread into the sauce to find out if it is sweet. And when Concetta has her back to him, he might also sneak a just-fried meatball before it makes its way into the gravy.

But Concetta welcomes him, invites him in fact, to sit at the kitchen table when holidays are approaching—Easter and Christmas. Then she coaxes, encourages, and sometimes begs him to come into the kitchen and slice ends of sopressata, prosciutto (the cheapest cuts), and basket cheese for Pizza Rustica at Easter. At Christmas, he kneads dough, forms it into ropes, and slices it into pillowy struffole.

Maddelana loves her neighbors, godmothers, sisters, even sisters-in-law, caring for them when they're sick, making sure their grandchildren cross the street safely, and helping them shop. But in the kitchen, that love does not go far. She defends her own dish to the death. It is the absolute best in her opinion—and worthy of more superlatives. As a result, if she must share a recipe, she leaves out an ingredient or two. One of the few times any nonna provides a recipe intact is if the recipient is pregnant. No nonna, even Maddelana, can resist a chance to fulfill an expectant mother's yen, or *voglia*.

Aniella doesn't like working with her daughters in the kitchen. The young women studied home economics in high school and learned how to cook "American," bathing cauliflower and canned tuna in cream sauce. Aniella's answer to such dishes is a wave of the hand and a, "Bah!" Even so, she makes a *besciamella*, a traditional cream sauce (the same as the one her daughters learned at school) to gloss vegetable lasagna, brimming with mushrooms, spinach, and Parmigiano.

Giuseppina cooks without enthusiasm. To her, it's a job. But her dishes turn out to be spicy, tasty, near-perfect, even though she complains to her husband that cooking gives her a headache and that she can't wait to get out of the kitchen. She has no problem keeping her husband out of the kitchen. You will often find her waving her cigarette about, acting as if she is the perfect spouse (when she isn't complaining about her aches and pains). She speaks deferentially to her husband, "Yes, sir," "No, sir," "Anything you say, sir." Then does exactly as she pleases—all without advice from Betty Friedan.

The four agree to never set foot inside a restaurant, Italian or otherwise. Concetta's reason: "They're not clean enough." Giuseppina's reason: "The olive oil is spoiled." Aniella's reason: "Too much money for too little food." Maddelana's is the clincher: "I saw the waiter blow his nose."

All four eat their lunch standing over the kitchen sink, even though there is a table with four empty chairs in the room. Coffee is their morning pick-me-up, their afternoon cocktail, and their evening cordial. After dinner, they take a walk, a *passegiatta*, stopping at one another's houses for coffee. They recount the events of the day and throw a barb or two, usually at the absent Giuseppina, who did something to displease them that afternoon. Maddelana says, "She didn't use enough oil in frying her peppers." Still the three rally to her side the following morning when she needs help getting a grandson off to school.

THE CHURCH

As they trot along the Avenue, shopping bags brimming with fruits, vegetables, and impossibly long loaves of crisp bread, they bless themselves when the church bells toll (it's important to say a prayer for the deceased) and when they pass a church. They have taught their children and grandchildren to do the same.

Their devotion to the church is second only to their devotion to their families. Concetta loves to scrub the sanctuary floor, dust the Stations of the Cross, and arrange flowers for the altar. This is her wonderful, magical Friday afternoon—better than a matinee. She and the others socialize around the church, accompanying one another to novenas, Rosary Society meetings, novenas, confession, and more novenas.

Concetta, Maddelana, Aniella, and Giuseppina also attend wedding ceremonies. No need for an invitation. They believe as long as they're in church for confession, they have a right to stay and see the bride. The wedding is part of their Saturday routine. They scrub the stairs, sear a steak, and show up at church to atone and exclaim about the flower girl's dress, all before 6pm.

Aniella is devoted to the church, but she also indulges in her own "spiritual" activities. Her spirituality flirts with superstition in the interpretation of her dreams. She believes (or says she does) that a dream of a happy occasion, a wedding maybe, is sure to predict someone dying or suffering a tragedy. Of course, neither death nor tragedy has befallen Aniella, despite her recounting each morning the marvelous wedding reception she danced at in her dream.

When a grandchild is sick, Aniella practices her folk spirituality. She shows up at the bedside carrying a vial of *chrisma*, or holy oil. In Italian, she mutters a Hail Mary or the Lord's Prayer and makes a very elaborate sign of the cross on the patient's forehead. Does this speed the recovery? Only a doctor knows for sure. And, although she doesn't rely on the neighborhood folk healer, Aniella still hopes to discuss the grandchild's illness with her.

Not in keeping with the Church's teachings at all, Giuseppina has been known to extend her index finger and pinky, a symbol of the *mal'occhio*, or evil eye. She does this to wish ill on someone she either envies or dislikes. She is convinced that if she accompanies the hand gesture with a compliment about the target, something evil is sure to follow. All the nonnas know, of course, that a red ribbon or red string wards off the evil eye. They make sure that they pin red ribbons on a downy organdy-covered bassinette to keep a newborn safe from evil.

TAKING ON THE WORLD WITH A WAVE OF THE HAND

No matter what activity Concetta, Maddelana, Giuseppina, and Aniella are involved in, they use their hands, and it's not only when they're mincing, dicing, kneading, sewing, and gardening. Aniella passes her palm over the seat of a chair in a home she's visiting. Then she brushes her hands together to rid them of dust, real or imaginary, as she sits. If she's visiting another nonna's home, she does it while the hostess has her back turned.

Giuseppina enacts a drama to get teenagers to shut up in church., She holds her hand parallel to her mouth and bites her index finger—the nonnas' universal symbol for displeasure or worse. With a wave of a hand and a very audible, "Bah," she dismisses whatever displeases her.

Concetta and Maddelana squeeze freshly baked bread with such force that crumbs fall all around, forcing the baker to sell the loaves to them at a discount. They poke the meat the butcher is weighing, hold up a fish and smell it before the fishmonger wraps it, and remove "bad" outer leaves from a head of escarole while the vegetable man looks on. They crinkle waxed paper as they unwrap their grandchildren's sandwiches at a movie matinee, causing them to annoy the other patrons and attract the attention of the usher.

At home, they all use their hands to scrub floors, windows, walls, and vegetables. The Fuller Brush man is one of their most welcome visitors. He provides their much-loved scrubbing aids. To decide what's best to use to chase away dirt, Concetta and Maddelana sometimes spend 20 minutes talking about the merits of bleach—Aqua Lina, bought at the grocery store, versus Javel Water, delivered to homes. For relaxation, they iron clothes they have dipped in boiled starch and dried. Then they micromanage each pleat into submission, and no ruffle bears a crease.

THEIR ROUTINE

In spring, Concetta starts a garden indoors. In summer, she sits and crochets on a folding chair at the curb. In fall, a pristine front apron adds color to her unbuttoned black coat when she's on her way to clean the church. In winter, she waits for the price of a live Christmas tree to go down to fifty cents, then lugs it up the stairs to her apartment.

Long before the word will be born, Maddelana is a locavore—a master at city gardening—who can't wait to harvest her figs, tomatoes, and zucchini. A windfall of zucchini embraces her basil, where blooming tomato plants hover over the herb's tender leaves. Tendrils of all three push up between ragged slabs of pavement in the tenement's tiny yard. Her favorite squash is a lime-colored, satiny-skin squash called a *cucuzza*. The length of the squash is a point of pride. When Maddelana's garden produces a *cucuzza* as tall as a four-year-old, she commands the respect of the neighborhood.

Aniella puts affection and care into the booties she crochets for a new arrival, and in assembling for the new mother a basket of food that could feed 12. She reaches into her bank, a sugar bowl, for a two-dollar bill to place in a Mass card for a nonna whose mother passed away. She takes pride in a cake she bakes for a pastor's anniversary celebration. And she is quick to remind anyone within earshot that her grandchildren are the best.

Giuseppina sits sipping tea and smoking at the others' kitchen tables. She tries to determine exactly what is cooking from its scent, from the type of pot that holds the ingredients, and from its location. She is better at identifying pots of soup simmering atop the range than casseroles in the oven. But what she never does is ask directly for a recipe. Instead, when she returns home, she will gather the same ingredients and make the same dish successfully.

They are neighbors, wives, sisters, mothers, cooks, and best of all grandmothers. Some of the dishes they made with their Italian recipes. Some they mastered as Americans. All their recipes—and their stories—deserve to live on long past the twenty-first century.

SPRING

Hurry Up . . .The Bride's Getting Out of the Car!

The weekly viewing of the brides is the greatest sporting event in the neighborhood and the only one Concetta, Aniella, Maddelana, and Giuseppina sprint for. Just like baseball, football, and hockey, there is a season (actually two) for this activity—spring, with time out for Lent; winter, with time out for Advent. As predictable as pro boxing matches on TV every Friday night at 9, the ceremonies take place on Saturdays and Sundays between 4pm and 5:30pm.

The Saturday events attract the neighborhood nonnas more than the Sunday ones. With their kerchiefs firmly tied beneath their chins and their snug black coats hiding their house dresses, the ladies are going to be in church anyway, to go to their weekly confession. And after they say their penance—generally three Hail Marys suffice for the sins they have confessed—they finger their rosaries, sit back in the pew, and wait for the first strains of the Wedding March.

Now on this Saturday afternoon, Maddelana and Concetta are dashing down the long hill to the church. "Hurry up," Concetta says, "The bride's getting out of the car!" And Maddelana's short legs propel her forward until, exhausted, she follows Concetta into the church and joins Aniella and Giuseppina in their pew.

In that pause between the sprinters catching their breath and the confessors putting away their rosary beads, they spy granddaughters, nieces, and neighbors' teenage daughters sitting across from them, also crashing the ceremony. The girls, who are speaking quietly and laughing, are also wearing kerchiefs, but draped over their heads and tied behind the neck to hide metal rubber-tipped curlers.

To attract the girls' attention, "Pss-ss-st," Giuseppina says. As the girls turn toward them, Concetta, Aniella, and Maddelana join Giuseppina in motioning to the girls to pipe down. But the girls ignore them. Hearing an even louder "Pss-ss-st," the girls turn again and wave off the "keep quiet" gestures. This does not sit well with the ladies. And when next they catch the girls' eyes, all four make the menacing universal gesture. The girls stop talking.

It matters not at all that the nonnas have no invitation to this ceremony, or to the 35 or so others they attend during the year. By right of being parishioners and neighbors (even though this particular bride lives 15 blocks away), the nonnas believe they are entitled to attend. And following their example, so do the teenage girls.

The music begins. The bridesmaids, all in pastel colors (this is a spring rainbow wedding), accompanied by fellows in white tuxedos, make their way down the aisle; the maid of honor and best man follow. Then the flower girl approaches holding a small basket and sprinkling petals as she goes.

Forget how beautiful the bride is. Maddelana is focused on the flower girl. She can't contain herself. She cries tears of joy. Aniella's exclamations of *"bella, bella,"* ring out through the church. Concetta admires aloud the flower girl's dress, her hair, her all-around greatness. The teenagers turn to the nonnas; each girl makes the universal gesture. The nonnas stop talking.

The bride sweeps in on her father's arm. As soon he gives the bride away to the groom, activity in the nonna and teenage pews begins again. It's time for the nonnas to go home and cook dinner. It's time for the teenagers to go home and take the curlers out of their hair. As they walk up the hill, the talk turns to the wedding. Giuseppina is quick to say, "The bride didn't look so special."

"I know," says Concetta. "The only one who looked really good was the flower girl." They nod in agreement.

Each dusts her hands together, signaling the end of the event, and talk turns to dinner. They have sacrificed an hour of the three hours they usually spend preparing dinner. (That's three hours spread out over the entire day, beginning with the roasting of the peppers first thing in the morning.)

"Tonight, we have sausage and peppers," says Aniella.

"Good," says Maddelana, "Maybe I'll be making a bread salad."

Giuseppina proudly pulls herself up to her almost-five-foot height and says, "I don't have to cook tonight. My daughter invited me over." Giuseppina turns away, and Concetta waves her hand dismissively, glances at the others, and they share a grin.

SAUSAGE AND PEPPERS

Serves four

$\frac{1}{4}$ cup olive oil
2 cloves garlic, peeled, quartered
Salt
Freshly ground pepper
1$\frac{1}{2}$ pounds Italian green frying peppers, seeded, sliced into 1-inch strips
$\frac{3}{4}$ cup dry red wine
2 cloves garlic, peeled, quartered
1$\frac{1}{2}$ pounds Italian sweet sausage with fennel, cut into 1-inch slices
3 tablespoons flat-leaf parsley, minced

Over medium heat, in a large, shallow skillet, heat the oil, 1 clove garlic, salt and pepper; saute until the garlic is golden.

Add the peppers; cook undisturbed for 10 minutes. Stir; continue to cook for 15 minutes, stirring occasionally until peppers are golden brown. Set peppers aside.

In the same skillet, bring the wine to a boil; reduce heat to simmer. Pierce sausage; add sausage, 1 clove garlic, salt and pepper.

Simmer sausage until wine evaporates and sausage releases its own fat. Increase heat to medium-high. Sauté sausage, stirring occasionally, 15 minutes, or until golden brown and cooked through.

Transfer peppers and their juices to skillet with sausage. Over medium heat, stir well to release bits of sausage from bottom of pan. Simmer until all ingredients are heated through. Transfer to serving dish; sprinkle with parsley. Serve

BREAD SALAD

Serves four

One 1-pound loaf Italian country bread or ciabatta, cut into 1-inch cubes
1 tablespoon fresh oregano, minced, or 1 teaspoon dried
1 clove garlic, finely minced
Salt
Freshly ground pepper
$\frac{1}{4}$ cup plus 3 tablespoons olive oil
$1\frac{1}{2}$ pounds very ripe beefsteak or plum tomatoes, sliced into 1-inch pieces
1 small red onion, diced
4 tablespoons fresh basil, torn into shreds, or 1 teaspoon dried basil

Preheat oven to 350 degrees F.

On a rimmed baking sheet, toss together the bread, oregano, 3 tablespoons olive oil, garlic, salt and pepper.

Bake in preheated oven for 12 to 15 minutes, tossing occasionally, until bread cubes are golden. Set aside 20 minutes to cool.

In a large salad bowl, toss the $\frac{1}{4}$ cup olive oil with remaining ingredients. Add salt and pepper to taste. Cover bowl with plastic wrap; set aside for 20 minutes to allow flavors to blend.

Add bread cubes to salad bowl. Toss. Serve.

Toss Me a Salami:
The Football Wedding

The bride, Concetta's niece Caterina, looks beautiful as she enters the church basement for her wedding reception. Concetta, Aniella, Maddelana, and Giuseppina, decked out in blue silk dresses of varying designs and wearing feathery hats, follow the wedding party into the hall. They stand on the side watching the bride and groom dance their first dance as Mr. and Mrs. to a 78 recording of Frank Sinatra singing "Always."

Concetta wipes away a tear, and Giuseppina lights up a Chesterfield, which she has been waiting to enjoy since the ceremony ended. Next, it is the turn of the father of the bride to lead his daughter onto the floor and foxtrot to "Star Dust" blaring from a scratchy Artie Shaw recording. Soon all the young couples join them on the dance floor.

As the niece's dance ends, the nonnas wipe their eyes, sobbing (not as much, though, as they would at a funeral for a brother-in-law).

And the dance? It signals the end of the romantic portion of the reception and the beginning of the frantic.

Maddelana is first in line. "Oh, everything looks so nice," she says to Giuseppina, who follows her.

"Yes," Giuseppina agrees. "But there don't seem to be enough ashtrays." The other guests fall in line; they all head in the same direction—to a table in the front of the room. The table overflows with waxed-paper-wrapped sandwiches, plates of celery, olives, olive salad, cheese, gallon bottles of red wine, pitchers of beer, bottles and bottles of grape, lemon-lime, cream, and orange local soda, towering pyramids of cream puffs, and cellophane-covered trays of cookies. In the center of the table rests a three-tier wedding cake. Atop the cake stand a miniature bride and groom under a heart-shaped wire canopy covered with artificial flowers. Surrounding the base of the cake are tulle-wrapped bunches of Jordan almonds.

As those in front make their way to the table, they hear an occasional shout from a guest at the end of the line: "Toss me a salami." Aniella, now in the front of the line, carefully examines a sandwich. "This isn't right; it's prosciutto." She shouts to the fellow asking for the sandwich. "Hold your horses, I'm working on it." She inspects another sandwich or two until one turns up that is filled with salami, and she tosses the sandwich to the fellow who requested it—a traditional food-distribution system at a football wedding.

As the reception progresses, Concetta dances with a toddler grandchild hanging onto her neck. Aniella stands guard over the sandwich table, identifying for the guests the filling of each sandwich.

Maddelana sits at a table with her sister Giuseppina. "Very nice, these sandwiches," she says.

"Yeah, but the olive salad is better," Giuseppina says. "I'll take a few sandwiches home anyway. This way I won't have to cook tomorrow." She starts clapping her hands to the rhythm of the music blaring from the turntable. "That sounds like a Neapolitan tarantella."

"No, I'm sure it's a Calabrese one," Maddelana says.

"I know for sure it's not a Sicilian one," Aniella chimes in. "But we should get up and dance anyway—for the bride."

They join Concetta on the dance floor.

Each nonna shows her stuff as she dances. Maddelana and Concetta link arms. Aniella and Giuseppina, with hands around each other's waist, wave napkins over their heads. The four form a circle, lifting their clasped hands in the air.

The other guests, clapping and stamping their feet in time to the music, form a circle around the nonnas. The circle is broken when the bride and groom join in the center and all the nonnas make way for them. The dance ends, and the revelers are about to leave the dance floor when a familiar song begins.

The crowd remains assembled on the dance floor as Giuseppina, her voice as loud as that of a feast singer, shouts out, "Oh, Mama." The song describes a woman's dastardly fate if she marries a baker or a musician or a butcher or anyone else the audience can name. She breaks into song, and her voice triumphs over all the whistling, the clapping, and the suggestions for verses—the most bawdy in Italian, the most family-friendly in English.

In a calm-down moment, the bride and groom cut the cake. Concetta and her husband, Calogero, approach the table. "You sure you put the money in the envelope?" Concetta asks Calogero as he hands her the envelope.

"Bah, for sure," he answers. "You want me to open the envelope?"

Concetta gives him a gentle elbow to the ribs. At the table, Concetta hands a piece of cake to her husband but takes none for herself. She picks up a small bouquet of Jordan almonds, kisses the happy couple, and slips the cash-filled envelope into the bride's lace-trimmed satin purse.

Finished eating their cake and cream puffs and cookies, Maddelana, Aniella, Concetta, and Giuseppina return to the main table. There, they carefully remove many-times folded shopping bags from their purses. Quietly, very quietly, each goes about stashing leftover sandwiches, cookies, and candy into her shopping bag.

When they step outside the hall, Concetta opens her own shopping bag. "Giuseppina, I'll give you two salami sandwiches for one prosciutto," she says.

"But only if you give me a few cookies," Giuseppina replies. And the trading begins, with all four requesting at once what looks most desirable in the others' shopping bags.

OLIVE SALAD

Serves six

1 pound mixed pitted, cracked olives, including Sicilian, Nicoise,
Kalamata, and dried oil-cured

2 stalks celery, diced

2 scallions, or green onions, diced

1 carrot, peeled and shredded

1 red bell pepper, diced

$\frac{1}{2}$ cup olive oil

2 tablespoons red wine vinegar

Salt

Coarsely ground black pepper

Dash red pepper flakes

Combine all ingredients.

Refrigerate until ready to serve.

A Dinner Party

Concetta, Maddelana, Aniella, and Giuseppina are visiting Concetta's niece, Caterina, for the first time since the wedding. The bride has to entertain the elders by preparing a first-rate dinner for them.

Caterina is an accomplished hostess: friends love her cooking, enjoy her hospitality, and always eagerly look forward to visiting. But the nonnas are not her friends; they are her evaluators.

The appraisal begins as soon as they are about to sit down to cocktails. Aniella makes no effort to see if Caterina notices as she indulges in the chair-swiping ritual. They sit down. The party begins.

The nonnas dig into beautifully arranged platters of prosciutto, provolone, figs, olives, and melon. They launch into chorus mode.

Maddelana has the opening salvo, "Too stringy this prosciutto; it sticks in my teeth."

Concetta says, "These olives are very tasty, but a little bit salty."

The platters are emptying fast, when Giuseppina pipes up. "The figs are nice," she says, biting into her fourth—or maybe her fifth. "But I'm not supposed to eat seeds, didn't you know?" she asks accusingly as she lights another cigarette to join the other two in an ashtray.

Aniella, silent, keeps refilling her plate.

Saved by the oven bell, Caterina asks the guests to come to the table. They do, and each repeats the seat-dusting ritual. Conversation at the table is about—what else? Food.

"Which market in this neighborhood sells the best *ricotta salata*?" Concetta asks. She does not expect a reply because the others have yet to comment on provisions in this neighborhood—four blocks away from their own.

"Prices are really high around here," Aniella says. "I saw the price of broccoli rabe, beets, and celery when we passed the vegetable stand."

"Never mind the prices," Giuseppina says. "It's the cooking here that drives me crazy." She turns to her sister Maddelana. "You remember Jenny on the next block?"

"Sure, I do," Maddelana says. "What's wrong with her cooking?"

"She doesn't fry the meatballs before she puts them in the gravy." That last statement raises all the eyebrows.

Portions of eggplant parmigiana appear on each plate. Concetta raises her glass in a toast: "*Cent'anni.*" May you live a hundred years.

And that is the last word spoken for a very long time. A silence descends when they bring the first forkful of glistening cheese-enrobed eggplant to their lips. The silence is, well, frightening. Caterina is alarmed. Is the eggplant too stringy, too salty, or home to too many seeds?

As the nonnas use chunks of bread to shovel the vegetable on to their forks and to absorb the rich sauce, they seem to have no need to talk. Sigh. They ask for seconds, reach into the bread basket again, and appear to be in a miasma of contentment.

When the salad is passed around, the spell is broken. "This isn't the salad like your mother used to make," Concetta says.

"Wrong kind of vinegar," Maddelana says.

Giuseppina, who has trouble digesting onions and garlic, pushes the salad's scallions to the edge of her plate, all the while shaking her head.

"You really don't have to use this expensive oil in a salad," Aniella says.

It's soon time for espresso, anisette, and cookies. The guests find the coffee "a little bitter," according to Giuseppina.

The anisette? "Galliano, not Sambuca?" Concetta asks, surprised. And the cookies Maddelana grudgingly deems "pretty good."

Later the nonnas slip on their coats; they are ready to leave, bestowing kisses and hugs and even a mini-blessing on Caterina. The golden silence during the eggplant episode proves the party was a success. They cannot tell the hostess, though, how delicious the dish was. (No compliments here!) But they do tell their neighbors. Each says, "She makes parmigiana pretty good—just the way I make it."

EGGPLANT PARMIGIANA

Serves six

4 small Japanese or zebra eggplant, about 1 ½ pounds total

3 large eggs

3 tablespoons flour

Salt

Freshly ground pepper

½ to 1 cup plus 2 tablespoons olive oil, not extra-virgin

2 cloves garlic, quartered

1½ cups tomato sauce (homemade or store-bought)

4 tablespoons fresh basil leaves, thinly sliced, or 1½ teaspoons dried

1½ pounds fresh mozzarella, cut into ¼-inch slices

Preheat oven to 375 degrees F.

Wash eggplant well; using a peeler, strip off some of the skin, leaving a striped effect; cut eggplant crosswise into ¼-inch slices.

In a large bowl, beat eggs, flour, salt, and pepper together, forming a batter.

Stir eggplant slices into batter.

Preheat a large skillet over high heat; when skillet is hot, add enough olive oil just to cover the bottom of the skillet.

Reduce heat to medium. Sauté eggplant slices, without crowding, in batches until golden, adding more oil as needed.

In the meantime, in a nonreactive pan, sauté garlic in the additional 2 tablespoons of oil; sprinkle with salt and freshly ground pepper.

When garlic is golden, add tomato sauce.

Let sauce simmer about 10 minutes; stir in basil leaves.

In a nonreactive casserole, layer the ingredients.

Spread a few tablespoons of tomato sauce in the casserole; add slices of eggplant followed by slices of mozzarella; sprinkle with tomato sauce.

Repeat layering, ending with a layer of mozzarella.

Sprinkle sauce on top.

Bake 35 to 45 minutes or until bubbly and golden. Wait 10 minutes before serving.

In the Style of the Shoemaker

The nonnas cook using "a dash of this, a spoonful of that, and a pinch of whatever." So on a rainy spring day, it is surprising when they sit at Concetta's kitchen table and talk about recipes—American recipes—their daughters clip from newspapers and magazines.

"I don't like the ones that use butter, not olive oil," Concetta says. The rest nod knowingly while wrinkling their noses. The prospect of using a Northern Italian or French medium to brown chicken makes them shudder.

"We're lucky we can find all the things we need to cook right here," Maddelana says. "My daughter-in-law," she pauses, "the Irish one, she travels far to get what she needs to cook when her mother is coming to dinner."

"Well, she could just use vegetables and chicken," says Giuseppina brusquely. "They're popular with everybody—Irish, American—and there are a thousand ways to cook them."

"Back home, my mother made wonderful dishes—like chicken

cacciatore—with mushrooms, celery, onions, carrots, you name it."
Aniella's voice grows sentimental.

"My daughter fixed a dish the other night that I thought was going
to be cacciatore, but it turned out she was using a recipe from a ladies'
magazine," Concetta says.

"Bah!" Giuseppina adds as she tears the cellophane from a new pack of
Chesterfields. "Those magazines and newspapers try to give original
recipes, but the food never tastes the way it should."

"She made something called Chicken Scarpariello—in the style of the
shoemaker," Concetta continues. "My mother never served it. I'm pretty
sure it's an American recipe."

"Did you taste it?" Aniella asks.

"It was delicious," Concetta answers. "It was chicken on the bone
cooked with sausage, a little wine, and hot vinegar peppers." The nonnas
all snap to attention at the mention of hot vinegar peppers. "I always keep
a jar in the refrigerator," Maddelana says. "They're nice on an antipasto
plate."

"And they're good on a sandwich with mozzarella." Giuseppina coughs
as she lights a cigarette and tries to speak at the same time.

The rain is letting up. As they get ready to leave, Maddelana and Aniella
place their coffee cups in the sink. Giuseppina follows with her tea glass.

"I'm going to the butcher," Concetta says. "Does anybody need
anything?"

"I'm fixing chicken tonight, but maybe you can pick me up a pound of
sausage?" Aniella says.

"He keeps the vinegar peppers on the shelf," Maddelana says. "Buy me
a jar, please."

Soon, the nonnas are in their apartments making dinner. A very
distinctive aroma of vinegar and sausage wafts from every window.

The nonnas meet after dinner to walk to a novena together. Each
changes the subject when asked what she cooked for dinner—a recipe
from an American magazine, perhaps.

CHICKEN SCARPARIELLO

Serves six

2 tablespoons olive oil
3 cloves garlic, quartered
One 4-pound chicken, cut into 10 pieces
Salt to taste
Freshly ground pepper to taste
1 pound sweet sausage with fennel, sliced into $\frac{1}{2}$-inch rounds
4 to 7 hot cherry peppers in vinegar, drained, diced
1 cup dry white wine or dry vermouth
$\frac{1}{2}$ cup chicken broth

In a skillet large enough to hold ingredients in one layer, sauté garlic in olive oil until golden; remove garlic; set aside.

Add sausage to pan; sprinkle with dash of salt and liberally with pepper.

Brown sausage well; remove from pan; set aside.

In same pan, sauté chicken until crisp and golden all over; remove from pan; set aside.

Pour excess oil from pan; add diced peppers, including seeds; sauté until golden.

Add wine to pan and reduce by half; add broth; stir all scrapings from bottom of pan into the wine and broth.

Return all ingredients to pan, including garlic; bring to a boil.

Reduce heat to simmer; cover closely; simmer 30 minutes or until chicken is cooked through.

Remove sausage and chicken from pan; set aside.

Over medium heat, reduce sauce until it coats a spoon; pour sauce over chicken and sausage; serve.

Price Wars

The nonnas don't go shopping. In their own dialects, they "make shopping," and they make shopping a work of art. It is the haggler's art of wearing down storekeepers to get the best and freshest provisions for the least amount of money. These little women all in black, save for their printed-front aprons, look perfectly innocent. No con artist would leave the house in such an obvious get-up. As they trudge uphill, laden with heavy paper bags from each of the stores they've visited, they still have breath enough to tell one another the way they managed to score the day's take.

It begins with the escarole. "I told Nick the vegetable man this escarole doesn't look so good," Maddelana says. "I start taking off the outside leaves, one by one. I'm ready to put it back in the box, and he says to me, 'It's fifteen cents, but take it for a dime.'" "Sure," says Giuseppina. "After what you did to that head, he knew he wouldn't be able to sell it to anybody else."

"It's tough to find things that are just right," Aniella insists. "You got to be picky."

"Pretend a little too," Concetta says, "like I do at the butcher's." A nonna has no trouble squaring her conscience with her carryings-on. "He has this chopped meat on a tray in the showcase. I want chopped meat, but I want to know what he's chopping. I say to him 'A pound of sirloin, please.' When he takes out the steak, I say, 'Please chop that for me.'"

"You should have seen the look he gave you—as sharp as one of his knives," Giuseppina says.

"In the bakery, you know the baker is going to grate the day-old bread into crumbs and sell the crumbs, right?' Maddelana says. "So I ask him to sell me a loaf of day-old bread. I take it home and make my own bread crumbs. If I buy crumbs from him—fifteen cents. If I buy day-old bread—ten cents." The bundles she carries prevent her from dusting her hands together to show that she has bested the baker; instead, she juts out her chin.

They approach a corner and look in the window of the toy store. "New stuff," Aniella says. "The doll, she's very nice for my granddaughter." She enters the store.

The others follow. They pull bills out of change purses that were stuffed into their apron pockets. "For my grandson," Giuseppina says, directing the storekeeper to a modeled-to-perfection miniature fire engine.

Aniella asks for the doll and a rattle for her newborn grandson. Concetta says, "The kids are going to have so much fun with these!" Bills are handed over. Change is received. And never is heard a haggling word. Why?

Because these are for the grandchildren—the only justification for ever paying full price.

....

ESCAROLE WITH BEANS AND "BACON"

Serves four

1 large head escarole, thoroughly washed, cored, sliced into thin strips
3 quarts boiling water
1 tablespoon olive oil
½ pound guanciale, or pancetta (Italian bacon), diced
2 large cloves garlic, thinly sliced
1 can, 12 ounces, best-quality cannellini beans, thoroughly rinsed
   and drained
Red pepper flakes to taste
Salt to taste

Blanche escarole in the boiling water 2 minutes; drain, set aside.

In a large skillet over medium heat, warm olive oil; add diced guanciale; sauté until golden and crisp; remove guanciale from pan.

Add garlic, red pepper flakes, and sprinkle of salt to fat remaining in pan; simmer garlic until golden; remove garlic; set aside.

Add escarole, raise heat to medium high; cover pan; steam escarole, covered, 5 to 7 minutes, or until tender crisp.

Reduce heat to medium, stir in beans; simmer 5 minutes or until beans are heated through.

Return sautéed guanciale and garlic slices to pan; stir; serve.

A Semi-Private Bath

Friday after Concetta, Aniella, and Maddelana finish cleaning the church, they visit the fish market to buy dinner. Whiting, cod, calamari, sole, shrimp, scallops, mussels. Each nonna has to smell each piece to make sure it's fresh. When Concetta sniffs a fillet that is less than fresh, she wrinkles her nose and invites the others to take a whiff and join in her disdain. They bow their heads to get closer to the offending sole. Then Giuseppina waves her hand in front of her face to whisk away the odor.

Carrying their purchases in brown paper bags, they walk home. "Do you want to go see a movie tonight?" Aniella asks.

Giuseppina and Maddelana nod in agreement. "I stay home tonight," Concetta says. "You know on Fridays Sophia, Calogero's youngest sister, comes over to take a bath."

"The miserable landlord she has in that building," Giuseppina says, drawing mightily on a Chesterfield, "when is he going to get a bathtub in that apartment?"

"I don't mind that she comes over." Concetta says. She dusts her hands to close the subject. She does not want to hear a negative word about a favorite relative—even one that is a relative on her *husband's* side. "We have dinner, coffee, cookies. I help her when she tints her hair."

"Oh, and does she do the same for you?" asks Giuseppina, raising her eyebrows.

"You see me; I don't tint my hair," Concetta says and pats her greying perm. "But she's single and keeping company with Gino down the street. They go out every weekend. She has to look good."

As they start down the block, they run into Sophia—young, beautiful with long, long black curls covering her shoulders. They hug, they kiss, they greet one another. Each nonna says, "Remember me to your mother."

Soon soup simmers on a back burner waiting for the addition of fish, mussels, and clams, as Concetta talks with Sophia in the kitchen.

The young woman starts emptying a brown paper shopping bag. Sophia places on the kitchen table a bar of Yardley lavender bath soap, a one-piece printed playsuit with long pants, the requisite underwear, and a 78-rpm record. She holds up the record. "Look what I got: Billy Eckstine," she says. "We can listen to it after dinner, when you do my hair."

"Okay, but everybody will be home soon; I got to finish the soup," Concetta says. She turns to the sink, slices a thick piece of cod in two, scrubs the mussels and clams, then adds the fish and seafood to the pot.

Later, grandchildren, sons, daughters and their husbands gather with Sophia around the table. Concetta dishes out the steaming soup. It doesn't take long for the guests to mop their plates clean with a heel of bread.

Dishes finished, the guests leave. Concetta makes coffee, sets out a plate of cookies, and waits for Sophia to finish bathing.

Sophia wears the fresh outfit and a towel around her shoulders as she enters the room. "Put on the record," she says to Concetta.

Soon Billy Eckstine is proclaiming, "Everything I Have Is Yours," while Concetta pours the coffee. Giuseppina, Maddelana, and Aniella on their way to the movies, pause to hear the love song through an open window.

This is Friday night in South Brooklyn, where sweet things happen.

FRIDAY NIGHT FISH SOUP

Serves six

4 tablespoons olive oil
2 cups peeled, diced russet or Idaho potatoes
1 cup diced carrots
1 cup diced celery
1 cup diced onion
Salt
Freshly ground pepper
2 tablespoons tomato paste
4 tablespoons anisette or other licorice-flavored liqueur
$\frac{1}{4}$ cup dry vermouth
2 bay leaves
Sprinkle of red pepper flakes

1 teaspoon dried basil or 1 tablespoon fresh, chopped
2 to 3 quarts boiling water
1¼ pounds cod fillet, skinned, rinsed
3 dozen littleneck clams, well scrubbed
1 pound mussels, debearded and well-scrubbed
1 pound shrimp, peeled and deveined

Warm olive oil in large nonreactive pot; add vegetables; sprinkle with salt and pepper; sauté vegetables until golden, about 15 minutes.

Add tomato paste; sauté over low heat 10 minutes.

Add anisette and vermouth; reduce by half; add herbs and pepper flakes; cover all ingredients with three inches of boiling water.

Return to boil; reduce to simmer; partially cover; simmer 30 minutes, or until vegetables are tender.

Add cod; simmer 10 minutes; return soup to boil.

Add clams and mussels; return heat to simmer.

After 7 minutes, check if shellfish open; remove from shells; discard any that have not opened.

Add shrimp; simmer 5 minutes or until shrimp turn pink.

Return shelled seafood to soup.

Serve soup with crusty bread.

Across the Alley

The nonnas wash, iron, and pack clothing that their grandchildren have outgrown. "I'm getting this box ready for Italy," Concetta says when Maddelana stops by one spring afternoon.

"I went to the post office last week and mailed a package," Maddelana says. "It had some pretty nice stuff in it—shorts, shirts, and skirts. I hope the clothes fit our niece on the other side." Any relative who lives in Naples, Sicily, or Calabria is said to live "on the other side."

And now the clothes are reappearing on children "on this side," at the candy store, in the grocery store, and—most important—across the alley. Families from Italy, through the efforts of religious and civic organizations, are making their way from their war-torn villages to the States, to New York City, to South Brooklyn.

Concetta's grandsons round up the new arrivals for games of kick-the-can, johnny-on-a-pony, and old-fashioned tag. Horsing around requires no fluency in English. Older guys show the boys how to construct a scooter out of a fruit crate, a small slab of wood, and a set of skate wheels. Concetta's granddaughters welcome the new girls on the block to bounce a Spaulding, the squeezable, pink ball known in Brooklyn as a Spaldeen. They jump rope, and play pottsy—the Brooklyn name for hopscotch. Aniella's friends, nephews, neighbors, or cousins help the children's fathers find construction jobs. Like horsing around, the work requires no fluency in English.

It's different for the children's mothers, homebound, baffled by the language and too shy to ask for help. They sigh, relieved, whenever they meet even Giuseppina in a non-Italian store. And as curt as she is toward the other nonnas, she is a bundle of patience and believes her day is a good one if she can help a mother make sense of "making shopping."

Through the open windows, the words of *"Cuore 'Ngrata"* and other Neapolitan songs waft from the new arrivals' apartments across the alley. Concetta and company enjoy the serenade while they sip their afternoon coffee. Aniella's talk turns first to dinner. "I'm doing pork chops tonight."

Then their talk turns to the music and the Italian station and the programs the new families enjoy. "Maybe we should try the Italian station at night, even if the kids don't like it," Concetta suggests. But the others appear not to hear her as they rise, straighten their front aprons, and make their way home to start dinner.

That evening after the dishes are done and the front aprons put in the hamper, the alley is silent. Then, as if at a given signal, Italian songs fill the air. Concetta, Maddelana, and Aniella have each tuned their radios to the Italian station.

In Concetta's apartment, a surprised son-in-in-law, moved by the music, says, "Ma, this song—I heard that when we fought in Italy."

Throughout the alley, the music continues very late into the night.

The following day, the nonnas meet on the corner on their way to clean the church. Each has listened to the entire show the night before, but no one brings it up. Instead, they talk about the weather.

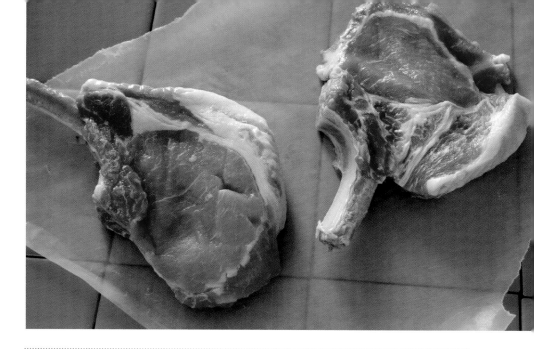

PORK CHOPS WITH WINE AND SAGE

Serves four

6 loin or rib pork chops, $\frac{3}{4}$-inch thick
6 tablespoons flour
Salt
Freshly ground pepper
3 tablespoons olive oil
2 cloves garlic, quartered
8 fresh sage leaves, or $\frac{1}{4}$ teaspoon dried
1 cup dry white wine

Mix flour with salt and pepper; dredge chops in seasoned flour.

Heat olive oil in large skillet; saute garlic until golden and remove from pan; set aside.

Brown chops until golden on each side; remove from pan; set aside.

Turn off heat; add wine; over medium-high heat simmer until wine is reduced by half.

Return pork chops and garlic to pan; cover; simmer 15 minutes, or until cooked through; serve.

Palm Sunday

Palm Sunday afternoon. Palm fronds cover Concetta's kitchen table where Maddelana, Giuseppina, and Aniella sit weaving strands into sculptures. They twist and braid and tie the green-edged leaves into crucifixes, wreaths, and miniature crosses, admiring one another's braiding technique, but never saying so. It's not their style to pay compliments.

"Now we finish these," Aniella says, holding up a cross that seems to be made of folds of ribbons. "Tomorrow we bring them to the cemetery and decorate the graves. And then I have to get busy shopping for the baking."

"Before I start the baking," Maddelana says, "I'm putting this wreath above the St. Teresa picture in my bedroom."

Giuseppina raises her eyebrows. "Bah," she says. "It's going to collect so much dust."

Concetta's husband, Calogero, is on his way out. As he walks past the table, he glances at the women's work. He picks up a miniature cross, two tiny strips of palm inserted one into the other, and slips the cross into the grosgrain band of his fedora; it adds a jaunty touch to the dark brown felt.

"You can help with the baking Wednesday night?" Concetta asks him.

"Sure," he answers as he makes his way to the door.

Once talk of the baking starts, it does not stop. The nonnas' kitchen capers—second only to their seven-fishes act at Christmastime—reach a crescendo at Eastertime with the baking of the chock-full-of-everything pizza rustica.

"You got some people to help you?" Maddelana asks her sister Giuseppina.

"Yes, even my Irish daughter-in-law says she'll help." Her reply meets with the nonnas' sly grins and delicate eye-rolling.

The baking begins days before Easter on Spy Wednesday, the night Judas Iscariot betrayed Jesus.

In Concetta's kitchen, as in every nonnas' kitchen on baking night, an enamel-top dining table overflows with chunks of Genoa and Sicilian salami, hot and sweet sopressata, dried fennel sausage, heels of prosciutto, balloon-shaped ovals of scamorza, wedges of Fontina and Asiago, and balls of fresh and smoked mozzarella. There is also the once-a-year specialty, basket cheese, dripping whey on a folded kitchen towel alongside a perforated tin of creamy ricotta.

It is time to make pizza rustica.

Concetta commands her daughter-in-law, "Hurry, beat the eggs in the big bowl." The younger woman begins beating and makes a face when her mother-in-law turns away. "You," Concetta shouts to two grandsons, "get busy on the cheese." The boys begin to dice the cheese and occasionally form bits into balls and lob them at each other when the grown-ups are out of sight.

On this evening, Calogero, a juice glass full of red wine at his side, sits at the head of the table carefully dicing the meats into half-inch cubes. "You, stop playing with the cheese," he addresses the boys. "If I throw a piece of prosciutto, you're going to be black-and-blue-for a week." The nonnas buy only the heel-ends of the prosciutto because they're cheaper. Those dried hunks could easily serve as weapons.

Bustling about, Concetta reminds the sous chefs that she is in a rush. "Everything has to be finished by tomorrow," she says. "I need the time to visit the seven churches."

"I know, I know," her husband says, "and then Good Friday, three hours more in church." He dismisses the whole deal with a wave of his hand.

At last, the pie is assembled. Concetta brushes the top with beaten egg for a gloss, makes a sign of the cross atop the baking pan, and puts the pan in the oven.

There is no eating the finished pie until Holy Saturday after the Mass of the Resurrection, the official end of Lent. With the Alleluias still ringing in their ears from the glorious Mass, the nonnas rush home to cut the pie, wrap individual pieces in waxed paper, and pack them in brown paper lunch bags.

They dispatch grandchildren in pairs to deliver slices to nonnas, uncles, aunts, and friends. The children do not have far to go: sisters live floors away from sisters-in-law in four-story buildings. Cousins can call out of windows to cousins. Aunts are a fire-escape climb away. No one has to travel more than three blocks to make a delivery.

The grandchildren return clutching a cache of slices from nonnas, uncles, aunts, and friends. Then the critique of the other pies begins.

"This pie is too salty," Concetta says.

That pie is too sweet. This crust is too thick. That crust is too thin. The verdict in each nonna's household: Her pie is the best.

PIZZA RUSTICA

Serves 12 as a main course; serves 24 as an appetizer

CRUST
4½ cups unbleached flour
¾ teaspoon salt
3 sticks ice-cold unsalted butter, diced
½ to ⅔ cup ice water

Combine flour and salt; place in food processor or electric mixer at low speed; work butter into flour mixture to form coarse crumbs.

Gradually add enough ice water to form dough that just sticks together.

Wrap dough in waxed paper; refrigerate while preparing filling.

FILLING
3 cups whole-milk ricotta, well drained
6 large eggs
Freshly ground pepper to taste
¼ pound prosciutto
¼ pound Genoa salami
¼ pound hot sopressata salami
¼ pound sweet sopressata salami
¼ pound Sicilian salami
¼ pound dried Italian sausage
¼ pound scamorza
¼ pound fresh mozzarella
¼ pound smoked mozzarella
¼ pound Fontina cheese
¼ pound Asiago,
½ pound basket cheese, well drained

GLAZE
1 egg yolk, beaten with 1 tablespoon milk

Preheat oven to 375 degrees F.

In a large bowl, beat together ricotta, eggs, and black pepper; set aside in refrigerator.

Dice remaining filling ingredients into $\frac{1}{2}$-inch cubes; stir into ricotta mixture.

Divide dough in two, with one piece slightly larger than the other.

On a lightly floured board, roll out larger piece and fit it into a (approximately) 12-inch-by-16 -inch nonreactive shallow casserole; leave an overhang of 1 inch.

Roll second piece of dough to fit over top; set aside.

Moisten the edge of the bottom crust with water; add the meat and cheese filling. Pour ricotta mixture over meats and cheeses.

Add top crust; crimp edges of crust together; flute edges; brush top crust with egg glaze; cut a circle in top crust to allow steam to escape.

Place casserole on baking sheet; bake 90 to 115 minutes or until the tip of a knife inserted into the center comes out clean.

Cool on wire rack.

Allow to come to room temperature before slicing; serve at room temperature; refrigerate leftovers

A Barley vs. Grain Spat

Holy Thursday, twilight is descending as the nonnas leave the seventh and last church they visit. They are eager to return to their neighborhood to shop for an essential ingredient—dried grain, or wheat kernels—for the pastiera, the sweet Easter pie.

"I'm getting the dried grain," Concetta says. "I'll soak it and bake the pie Saturday afternoon."

"I'm buying mine soaked," Aniella says. "It's much easier that way, even though I still have to cook it." The others shake their heads slowly in disapproval.

"Easy, easy?" Giuseppina says. "I make the pie the easiest. I use barley, the medium size, not too small. Boil it, simmer it, cool it, and I'm ready to go."

The others gasp audibly. "No wheat?" Concetta exclaims. "Just barley?"

"Oh, yes," Maddelana says, poking a bit of fun at her sister. "It's more modern."

"Last year, when you tasted the pie did you think it was bad?"

There is a reluctant "no" from Maddelana. But Aniella and Concetta shrug their shoulders and roll their eyes at each other. How could they have missed an opportunity to find something a little "off" in someone else's baking?

"Oh, yes," Giuseppina says. "I follow the old recipe, but using barley saves me time."

They enter the local pastry shop, and each places an order for orange flower water, vanilla sugar, and diced citron. All but Giuseppina order wheat dried or soaked.

"Signora, some grain for you—dried, soaked?" the shop owner asks

Giuseppina after he organizes each nonna's purchases on the counter.

"Oh, no thank you," she says. "I have what I need already."

"You're not using some left over from last year, are you?" the shop owner asks, aghast.

"Bah," Maddelana answers. "She's using barley." She spits out the word like an epithet. She shakes her head. "Too bad we don't keep the old traditions."

"If it tastes as good with barley, what's the difference?" Giuseppina says. "Tradition is in the taste."

Concetta, Maddelana, and Aniella arrive at their apartment building and bid one another good-night. Soon the sound of dried grain pings as Concetta pours it into a bowl and sets it to soften overnight. The following day, she simmers the soaked grain and refrigerates it until baking day, Holy Saturday.

While the grain is simmering in Concetta's kitchen, Maddelana and Aniella are at the kitchen table having coffee. Giuseppina stops by to ask if they want her to pick up anything from the stores.

"I have nothing to do right now," Giuseppina says with a glimmer in her eye. "I don't fix the barley until tomorrow when I'm ready to bake the pie."

"Barley!" Maddelana says almost to herself. "No, I don't need anything, thanks," she says, even as she realizes she really could use a dozen eggs, some butter, more sugar.

The day of reckoning arrives. The nonnas' kitchens are filled with the sweet scents of oranges, vanilla, and buttery crusts. Each works swiftly to chill the finished pie for serving at Easter breakfast.

While they wait for their pies to cool, they gather around the kitchen table in Giuseppina's apartment. She places her half-smoked cigarette on the edge of the sink and hands out cups of steaming espresso and thin slices of cooled pastiera—her pastiera.

Waiting to hear the verdict, she busies herself at the sink. Soon she hears Concetta say, "Very nice, the vanilla and the lemon."

"Oh, it does taste just like the one Mamma used to make," Maddelana says.

Aniella says, "It tastes just like mine!" Giuseppina continues her work at the sink with her back to the guests, and she does so wearing an ear-to-ear grin.

PASTIERA—EASTER GRAIN PIE

Serves eight

CRUST

2¼ cups unbleached flour

2 sticks very cold unsalted butter

½ teaspoon salt

¼ cup sugar

2 large egg yolks

⅛ to ¼ cup ice water

FILLING

½ cup wheat grains, soaked overnight; or ¾ cup medium barley kernels

3 cups water

Dash salt

1½ cups whole milk

3 tablespoons sugar

Grated rind of 1 orange

3 cups whole milk ricotta, drained

1½ teaspoons pure vanilla extract

Grated rind of 1 lemon

3 large eggs

½ cup sugar

¼ teaspoon salt

2 tablespoons orange flower water
1 tablespoon dried citron, diced (optional)
GLAZE
1 large egg yolk beaten with 1 tablespoon milk

For grain: Soak dried grain 24 hours.
Rinse soaked grain; bring to boil in 3 cups water.
Simmer grain, covered, 40 minutes or until tender and all liquid is absorbed.

For barley: Simmer 40 minutes in 3 cups water, or according to package directions, until tender and all liquid is absorbed.

For pie: Warm milk with sugar, salt, and orange rind. Add milk mixture to cooked grain or barley; simmer until liquid is absorbed; allow to cool.

In an electric mixer with a whisk attachment, beat together the remaining filling ingredients until light; fold in grain.

Crust

In a food processor or electric mixer, blend together all ingredients for crust. Add more ice water if dough is too dry; wrap dough in plastic wrap and chill 1 hour.

Preheat oven to 375 degrees F.

Divide dough into two pieces, one piece slightly larger than the other. Roll the larger piece of dough to fit into and cover the sides of a 10-inch springform pan or deep pie dish.

Roll remaining dough; cut into 1-inch strips for lattice to top the pie; set aside.

Pour filling into crust; weave lattice on top; brush with glaze.

Place dish on baking pan; bake 90 minutes or until puffed and golden brown.

Allow to cool in turned-off oven.

Chill well before removing from pan; serve at room temperature; refrigerate leftovers.

New Spot for a Garden

The groundwork for an exodus begins on a sunny springtime late Sunday afternoon when Concetta's daughter invites her mother to join her family for a ride. With the dinner dishes put away after the big meal and the remaining jam-filled *crostata* back in the refrigerator, Concetta accepts. In the car, she takes her place between her bickering 12-year-old grandson and his 10-year-old sister.

"I'm sitting in the middle," she says, "because I don't want you to kill each other."

They are quiet for a minute. Then, as she leans forward, they make ugly faces at each other behind her back.

"I know what you're doing," Concetta says. "That's the end of it."

She sits back to enjoy the ride, never thinking to ask where the driver, her son-in-law, is heading. After about an hour, he parks the car in front of a Cape Cod-style house with a sign on it reading: Model Home.

The boy runs to open the door. As Concetta and the family enter the living room, she sees other visitors—all couples around the age of her daughter, all with children racing around, grumbling, sometimes smiling. Her son-in-law leads the way. They walk through the kitchen with its shiny big window and gleaming appliances. They enter the master bedroom with windows set high enough to guarantee privacy. The children start to quibble as they approach a small corner bedroom.

"This is the room I want," the boy says.

"No, I want this one for myself," the girl says.

As they end the tour in the living room, with its small bay window, it dawns on Concetta that this is no simple Sunday excursion. Her apprehension is confirmed when her son-in-law approaches a man sitting at a desk in the living room. The man hands him a brochure and begins reciting a set speech about how safe the streets here are for children, how wonderful it is that the house comes equipped with new appliances, and how a sprinkle of grass seed is going to produce a magnificent lawn.

Concetta wonders if her daughter is planning on moving into a house like this with its clay lawn and shingle siding on a flat, flat street. She wonders if she is ever going to have a chance to walk the grandchildren to school again. And if her daughter is ever going to call for her so they can walk to a novena together on Wednesday nights.

When they return to the car, Concetta is twisting her handkerchief in her hands. She listens closely as her daughter points out all the advantages of living in Levittown. Her son-in-law? Not so much. He complains about the distance of the commute to his job, the fact that most of their furniture won't fit in the "dinky" rooms.

The couple in the front seat continues to discuss the pros and cons of a move. The children join in. "I said I wanted that room, but I really don't want to leave my friends," the boy says. "And I like my teacher so much this year," the girl says. "I don't want to change schools."

Concetta, fingers crossed beneath the knotted handkerchief, begins to relax. So maybe they won't buy a house and move now. But she stops a tear from falling as she realizes it is only a matter of time—not only for her daughter and her family, but also for all the daughters on the block.

CROSTATA MARMELLATA—JAM TART

Serves eight

CRUST
$2\frac{1}{4}$ cups unbleached flour

1 teaspoon salt

2 sticks very cold unsalted butter, cut into 1/2-inch dice

$\frac{1}{2}$ cup sugar

2 large egg yolks

$\frac{1}{4}$ to $\frac{1}{3}$ cup ice water

Mix flour, salt, and sugar together. Cut butter into flour mixture until mixture resembles coarse corn meal.

Work egg yolks and a small amount of iced water into mixture, forming a soft, smooth dough. Wrap dough in plastic wrap; refrigerate at least 1 hour.

FILLING
1½ cups cherry or apricot jam

GLAZE
1 large egg yolk
1 tablespoon milk

Preheat oven to 350 degrees F.

Roll out dough to ¼-inch thickness; cut in two, one piece larger than the other.

Fit larger portion into 9-inch tart pan with a removable bottom.

Slice remaining dough into 1-inch strips to use for lattice to top tart.

Spread jam over crust in pie pan; place strips of lattice on top.

Blend egg yolk with milk; brush lattice to glaze.

Place pie on rimmed cookie sheet or jellyroll pan to prevent spills.

Bake in lower third of oven 1 hour, or until jam is bubbling and crust is golden.

Cool on wire rack.

FOR LEFTOVER DOUGH
Place leftover lattice slices on cookie sheet around tart pan.

Brush slices with glaze; sprinkle lightly with sugar.

Bake 20 minutes, or until golden.

Remove to wire rack to cool while tart continues baking.

A Live Show

For the nonnas, Saturday morning shopping is more challenging than their daily stop at the vegetable stand, butcher shop, or fish market. On Saturday, Concetta, Maddelana, Aniella, and Giuseppina go to the live-poultry market, a.k.a. the chicken market, grandchildren in tow. Their parents have a morning to themselves. "My daughter is going to clean the house," Aniella says.

"What, she's not going to spend some time at the beauty parlor?" Giuseppina asks. "Whenever I take the kids, their mother rushes off to get a permanent or a new hair color," she says about her daughter-in-law. "But what are you going to do? She's Irish."

Inside the market, each selects a lively, sleek white bird. Maddelana raises her voice, warning the children, "Stay away from that coop, he's a mean rooster, and he'll peck your fingers."

The nonnas don't have to worry about the children's safety. The children are looking out for themselves. Each child, nose tightly clasped between thumb and index finger, hides behind a nonna. But the sight of chickens running around with their heads cut off and the smell of singed feathers do not interfere with Concetta's haggling over the price and weight of the perfect bird.

Purchase completed, ordeal over, the kids race up the block to the *pasticerria* for their promised lemon ice. The nonnas are involved in talking about their new fowl finds. "Oh, did you see?" Aniella asks. "The market is now selling ducks."

"Too expensive," Maddelana says. The others nod in agreement. "I'm thinking about how I'm going to roast this chicken. It's pretty big, four pounds."

"Yes, but it doesn't have as big a breast as mine has—more white meat," Giuseppina says, lighting up a Chesterfield and smiling proudly.

"I can't wait to get home to clean out this bird," Concetta says. "Maybe I'll find an egg yolk. It brings good luck. My mother used to find one inside almost every bird she cleaned."

"I remember once my mother was so lucky," Aniella says. "She found a double, bright yellow yolk." This ends all further talk of yolks. No one else's mother has ever had such luck.

"I'm not sure I bought a big enough chicken," Concetta says. "Maybe I should have bought two."

Maddelana reassures her. "As long as you serve it after the soup, the pasta with the gravy meat, and the vegetables—along with the roast potatoes—you'll have more than enough." They all nod, relieved. "That's what I do," she says.

Each returns a child, sticky with lemon ice, to a mother.

At home, the nonnas wash, trim, and ready the birds for their roasting on the following day. They hack toenails off feet, turn gizzards inside-out, trim knobby wings, preparing all to join the vegetables and the leftover bones from the roasted Sunday bird for a Monday soup.

Now picking, probing, pulling, and rinsing, each nonna cleans a chicken to her satisfaction. But to Concetta's dismay, there's not an egg yolk in sight. Better luck next time.

ROAST CHICKEN

Serves four

One 4-pound roasting chicken
2 lemons, halved
2 tablespoons balsamic vinegar
1 tablespoon olive oil
6 garlic cloves, quartered
1 bunch fresh rosemary
Salt
Freshly ground pepper

Preheat oven to 400 degrees F.

Rub chicken inside and out with the halved lemons; place lemon halves in cavity of chicken.

Mix vinegar and oil; rub chicken inside and out with mixture

Separate the skin from the flesh by running your fingers underneath the skin; insert garlic slices under legs, thighs, breast, back, and inside cavity.

Insert branches of rosemary alongside the garlic under skin and inside cavity.

Rub chicken inside and out with salt and pepper

Place chicken breast-side down on rack in roasting pan; roast 1 hour.

Turn chicken breast-side up on rack in roasting pan; roast 45 minutes, or until juices run clear and leg moves freely in its socket.

Place chicken on plate; remove lemons, garlic and rosemary from cavity and discard; tent chicken with foil; let rest 15 minutes before carving.

Saturday at the Movies

On weekends, the nonnas often take the grandchildren to the movies. One Saturday, Concetta, Giuseppina, Maddelana, Aniella and their grandchildren enter a local theater. The children laugh as they race down the aisle. Even though it's ten minutes until the feature begins, the matron stops them. Her flashlight beam would be at home reflected on a prison wall.

"Leave the kids alone," Aniella says, warding off the beam of light with her open palm.

"Go watch those kids in the balcony," Giuseppina says, "Smoking!" She lowers her voice. "I wish I was with them." She sighs. "What are they, eleven years old?"

The matron adjusts her hairnet, points the flashlight at the floor, and races up the stairs to the balcony.

The nonnas have as much trouble keeping their voices down as the grandchildren do. "I never sit in the balcony," Concetta says. "All that smoking. Bah! "

"Shh, quiet!" says a woman sitting in the row behind them.

"Eh," Maddelana addresses her. "It's only the coming attractions," she says. "We stop talking when the movie starts." She waves her hand in the air.

"I used to go to the movies only when it was Dish Night," Aniella says. "That set in my china closet? I got each piece at Dish Night just for the price of a ticket."

"Oh, Dish Night, those were some movies," Concetta says. "Fred Astaire, Ginger Rogers, Spencer Tracy," she pauses, "as a priest!"

"You want to see a real priest?" Giuseppina asks and answers her own question. "Bing Crosby in *The Bells of St. Mary's.*"

A man sitting in the row behind them warns them. "If you don't keep quiet, I'm going to call the matron—and then the usher!"

Now, right before the movie is about to begin, the kids are quiet. But the nonnas start crinkling waxed paper as they unwrap each sandwich and form the paper into little boat-shape holders for the children's lunch. They begin to distribute the food. "Here." "Eat." "Drink?" As they talk, the feature comes onscreen.

"Matron," the man in the row behind whispers loudly. The matron is unavailable because she's still trying to gain control of tobacco row in the balcony.

Silence descends.

When the movie is over, the newsreel comes onscreen. "You want to stay for the double feature?" Aniella asks.

"No, it's almost time to get to church and go to confession," Maddelana answers.

As they troop up the aisle, the chatter of the nonnas, the giggles of the grandchildren, and the rustle of the waxed paper from lunch elicit audible responses from the patrons in the aisle seats "shush,"—pleas for "quiet," and loud-enough-to-be-heard expletives.

"Oh," Maddelana points to the keep-quiet crowd. "You people are so rude."

In the light of day, all, including the nonnas, use their outside voices—their everyday shouting voices—to discuss the movie, the time they'll meet at church, and, of course, the dinner menu.

It's a given: on most Saturday nights, the nonnas serve an American meal—steak and potatoes.

"Tonight," says Concetta, "I'm making steak, but steak pizzaiola."

The others are impressed. One, it's cheaper than sirloin. Two, they kick themselves for not thinking of it first.

STEAK PIZZAIOLA

Serves four

1½ pounds shoulder, top round, or chuck steak, 1¼ inches thick
Sprinkle oregano
Sprinkle salt
Sprinkle red pepper flakes
3 tablespoons olive oil
½ cup diced onions
2 garlic cloves, quartered
3 large ripe tomatoes, seeded, diced
1 bay leaf

Preheat oven to 325 degrees F.

Dry steak on paper towels. Rub meat thoroughly with oregano, salt, and red pepper flakes.

Over medium heat, in a large oven-proof skillet, sauté garlic until golden in 1 tablespoon olive oil. Remove garlic; set aside.

Brown steak on all sides in the garlic-flavored oil; set aside browned meat.

Add remaining olive oil to pan; sauté onions until golden. Add tomatoes, bay leaf, salt, freshly ground pepper, and another sprinkle of oregano.

Sauté tomatoes about 7 minutes until they are softened.

Return steak to skillet; add reserved garlic.

Spoon sauce over meat; bring to boil; cover; place in oven.

Bake 1½ to 2 hours, or until meat is fork-tender.

Let rest 15 minutes before slicing and serving.

The Saint's Big Day

The young mothers lean out their windows as they hear the band approaching. They rest their elbows on pillows on the windowsill. They each share the space with a child and clutch a nickel or a dime, or a handful of change to toss into the trays of the girls collecting for the feast. They wave to one another and offer opinions to their neighbors in adjoining windows as to when the parade will pass. "It will be here soon," a mother says, "maybe a couple of minutes more."

The sound of the tubas coming closer makes the children giddy. "Be careful," a mother says, "you'll fall out the window."

Finally, the men who collected for this celebration—march into view. Each wears his best suit with a "committee" button pinned on his lapel. The brass band follows.

Eight young men carry the statue of the saint on a paper-flower-bedecked platform as it makes its way behind the band. The priest leading the statue walks mostly backward so he can bless the saint every now and then. On the sidewalk, teenage girls in frilly pastel dresses hold trays to collect coins raining from windows.

Members of various church organizations march behind the saint. And finally in the last group, the Rosary Society, are Maddelana, Giuseppina, Aniella, and Concetta marching in their no-nonsense oxfords. Each clutches a rosary and periodically makes an elaborate sign of the cross, ending with a kiss on a finger raised in the direction of the statue. All the while, they are talking about the best way to prepare porchetta, a roast of pork.

"Mamma, Mamma," the ladies in the windows shout. "Nonna, nonna," the children join in. And the nonnas can't help acknowledging them. "Giuseppina get out of my way," Maddelana urges. "I have to wave to the kids." Concetta elbows Aniella to make sure that she sees the greeting Concetta receives from her grandchildren who are framed in a second-story window. The nonnas interrupt their discussion about the roast.

Then Concetta's smile fades as a perceived injustice dawns on her. "Look," she says, "the kids from the grammar school are closer to the front than we are. And to the saint!"

"The Sodality is walking almost right behind the saint!" Maddelana says as she pauses to make a quick sign of the cross, followed by an elaborate kiss. "There are too many groups in front of us. We should be closer to the Saint, not following *every* group."

"We're the Rosary Society," says Giuseppina. "I wouldn't mind if we followed the Sodality, but we're following the Holy Name Society. We're walking behind the men's group!"

Aniella angrily crosses herself, offers the requisite kiss, and waves a silencing hand to her grandchildren who continue to call to her from the window. "We have to move up next year," she says. "My husband is on the committee. We get together and we ask him. Okay?"

They are silent for a while until the scent of a generously herbed pork roast wafts from a first-floor window. "And if he doesn't agree . . ."

Giuseppina interrupts Concetta, "No porchetta for him!"

PORCHETTA OR ROAST PORK

Serves six

One 4-pound boneless pork loin, tied with butcher's twine

Ingredients for the rub
1 tablespoon salt
1 teaspoon freshly ground pepper
2 teaspoons fennel seeds
1 tablespoon grated lemon rind
1 tablespoon grated garlic,

Ingredients for the herbs
6 sprigs fresh sage
6 branches fresh rosemary
6 sprigs fresh basil

Ingredients for the gravy
6 tablespoons flour
2 to 2½ cups water
¼ cup heavy cream
Salt
Freshly ground pepper

Preheat oven to 375 degrees F.

Dry pork; set aside 10 minutes.

Chop the rub ingredients together; rub into pork.

Place pork fat-side-up on a rack in a roasting pan.

Insert herbs—stems and all—under the twine on the roast.

Roast 2 hours, or until a meat thermometer registers 165 degrees.

Remove roast to serving platter; cover loosely with foil for 15 minutes. Slice; top with gravy.

GRAVY

Stir flour into drippings in roasting pan; simmer 8 minutes.

Add water; stir to dislodge bits left on roasting pan; simmer 5 minutes.

Add cream; simmer 5 minutes; serve.

It's All In a Name

Ah, May… the month of Mother's Day, the month of Our Lady, of communion breakfasts, of the bishop's annual visit to the parish church—and the month for Confirmation and selecting another name.

Today Concetta, Maddelana, Giuseppina, and Aniella are honoring Our Lady. They bring up the rear of a procession following grade-school girls dressed in white and wearing veils. The tallest eighth-grader leads the procession because she's tall enough to reach up and place a crown of flowers on the statue of Our Lady.

It's Mother's Day, and the nonnas, rosary beads twined around their knuckles, wear their traditional black. But today there are no front aprons. Instead each has pinned a carnation to her outfit. Concetta and Aniella wear white carnations. Their mothers are dead. Maddelana and Giuseppina, whose mother is still giving them grief, display pink carnations.

As the procession winds its way from the grade school to the church, the nonnas join in singing, ". . . we crown thee with blossoms today, queen of the angels. . . ."

When the hymn ends, Giuseppina nudges Aniella. "Look, the tall one carrying the crown. Poor girl, she'll never marry."

"She'll probably become a nun," Maddelana says quietly, looking pleased with the idea.

"Sh! Sh!" Concetta hisses. "Everybody will hear you. Besides, she might meet a really nice tall fellow." The gossips bow their heads and finger their rosaries.

It starts to drizzle when the procession reaches the churchyard. Suddenly there's an outpouring of prayers, rosary-bead clicking, and kisses to heaven. "Oh, the rain must not ruin the ceremony," Concetta says.

The nonnas' prayers to keep the rain away ascend like a Navajo chant. The invocations work, and the clouds remain just full enough to contain a real downpour.

The pastor's homily stresses how special mothers are. Throughout, the nonnas nod in agreement.

When the ceremony ends, they rush up the hill from the church. Aniella and Concetta must return later in the day to see the bishop confirm their grandchildren as soldiers of Christ. Though breathless as they climb, each talks about what she'll serve at the confirmation party.

"I'm going to do sandwiches—some pot roast I made yesterday on nice warm rolls," Concetta says.

"Me, too," Aniella says. "Sandwiches are perfect for a crowd. Who's your granddaughter's sponsor?'"

"Bah, my daughter is so modern. She doesn't believe in that. My granddaughter's sponsor is the one the pastor picks to stand up for all the kids who have no sponsor."

"That's okay," Maddelana says. "But what will she do about a Confirmation name? She'll have no one to name herself after."

"It's only a middle name—not so important," Concetta says. "But I think she likes Veronica."

"That's a good saint's name," Giuseppina agrees.

"What about your grandson?" Concetta asks Aniella. "Is he having a sponsor?"

"Yes, but there's a little disagreement," Aniella replies, shaking her head. "My son-in-law couldn't ask his younger brother Joe to be the sponsor because he's named after their father. If he were the sponsor, my grandson would be named Joseph Joseph."

"Of course," Concetta nods, understanding completely.

"When he asked his older brother Gaetano to be the sponsor, Joe had a fit," Aniella continues. "And now my grandson is complaining that he doesn't want Gaetano as a middle name."

"Maybe being modern is better," Concetta concludes. "No family fights."

STUFFATO OR POT ROAST

Serves eight

One 4-pound bottom round, or rump roast
4 tablespoons olive oil
1 large onion, sliced
2 medium carrots, peeled, diced
Salt
Freshly ground pepper
2 tablespoons tomato paste
1 teaspoon dried thyme
1 bay leaf
2 cloves garlic roughly chopped
4 tablespoons flour
6 to 8 cups dry red wine
8 or 10 Sicilian rolls for sandwiches (optional)

Preheat oven to 325 degrees F. Place rack in lower third of oven.

Heat a nonreactive Dutch oven or deep pot with cover; when pan is hot, add 2 tablespoons olive oil.

Dry meat well with paper towels, and sprinkle with salt and pepper; brown in pan on all sides; set meat aside.

Add remaining oil to pan and sauté onions and carrots until golden.

Toss flour into vegetable mixture; sprinkle with salt and pepper; sauté and stir over medium-low heat 5 minutes, or until golden.

Add tomato paste, thyme, bay leaf, and garlic to pot; sauté 4 minutes.

Add wine to vegetable mixture, simmer until wine is reduced and loses its alcohol scent.

Return meat to pot; liquid should come halfway up meat.

Bring to boil; cover; place in oven; baste and turn after $1\frac{1}{2}$ hours; continue baking 1 to 2 hours more, or until a fork pierces the meat easily.

Allow to rest 20 minutes before slicing and serving; refrigerate if made a day ahead.

Getting Sauced

The scent of simmering garlic, red pepper flakes, tomatoes, and fennel-seeded sausage fills the air as Maddelana hurriedly makes her way home from a Sunday nine o'clock Mass. The others had attended "the eight" (o'clock Mass, that is) and are already making tomato sauce ("gravy" as they call it) on kitchen stoves that rest next to organdy-covered open windows. The drainboards on the kitchen sink and the top of the kitchen table are their work stations—no counters here. Chop basil on a flat plate; squeeze tomatoes through a colander on the table; for meatballs, soften day-old bread under a cold running tap.

Concetta looks out a window and queries the scurrying Maddelana. "What happened? You couldn't wake up?"

Maddelana isn't in the mood for pleasantries. Muttering something about having "company late last night," she proceeds down the avenue.

But a nonna being late for Mass is a matter to take seriously. And so the shouting out the windows begins, with each nonna questioning the other as to why Maddelana couldn't rouse herself this morning. "And what will she do about the gravy?" Aniella asks.

"When her son and his family get there, the gravy won't be thick enough for them to dip a crust of bread in!" Concetta answers. "She lost an hour of cooking!"

As soon as everything is ready to remain unattended on the stove, Aniella, Concetta, and even Giuseppina—who happens to be walking past after buying her pack of Chesterfields—gather on the stoop in front of Concetta's tenement. They sniff and Concetta says, "Smell that? Maddelana's gravy is already going strong." They stop talking as Maddelana opens the door to join them.

"Oh, so hot in there by the stove," Maddelana says, wiping her hands on her flower-printed front apron.

The rest are eager to know about the "instant" gravy but are reluctant to ask. Finally, Giuseppina says, "What time is your son coming over today?"

Concetta joins in, "Will he have the kids and his wife with him?"

"Yes," Maddelana says to each of them.

Aniella clears her throat and asks, "How's the gravy going?"

"Good, nice and sweet."

The suspense is killing them. Giuseppina simply has to know. "But how did you make it so fast?"

"Yesterday I fried the meat," Maddelana says. "Today I add the tomato puree." She leaves to go in and stir the gravy.

Concetta shakes her head. "Tomato puree, bah."

The others nod in agreement.

"INSTANT" GRAVY AND MEATBALLS

Serves eight

The secret to this gravy is it takes only two hours, not four, to become perfect. The day before serving, prepare the meatballs.

Meatballs
3 slices white bread
2 large eggs
$\frac{1}{4}$ cup whole milk
2 cloves garlic, finely minced
3 tablespoons currants
2 tablespoons pine nuts
$1\frac{1}{2}$ pounds chopped sirloin
$\frac{1}{2}$ pound ground pork
Salt and pepper to taste
4 tablespoons olive oil

Douse bread with cold water; squeeze out water.

Mix together all ingredients except meat and olive oil.

Add meat; mix gently; shape into balls the size of walnuts.

Warm skillet over medium heat; add olive oil; sauté meatballs a few at a time without crowding them.

Place on paper towels to drain; refrigerate covered when they come to room temperature.

The following day, prepare the gravy.

GRAVY
1½ pounds sweet and hot Italian sausage, sliced into 2-inch pieces
2 cloves garlic, quartered
1 onion, thinly sliced
2 tablespoons olive oil
1 cup red wine
1 bay leaf
2 teaspoons dried basil
2 teaspoons dried rosemary
Sprinkle of red pepper flakes
1 can San Marzano tomatoes
2 eight-ounce cans tomato sauce
Sautéed Meatballs (see recipe above)

In a large, heavy nonreactive pot or Dutch oven, heat the olive oil.

Add sausage and garlic, brown thoroughly; add onion, brown; add wine; simmer until reduced by half.

Add remaining ingredients, except meatballs.

Bring sauce to boil; add meatballs; reduce heat.

Bring sauce to a simmer; partially cover pot; stir occasionally.

Simmer 2 hours, or until sauce is thick.

PASTA
1 pound dried pasta of your choice
5 quarts heavily salted cold water
½ cup Parmigiano Reggiano, grated in shards (optional)

Bring salted water to a rolling boil; add pasta; stir.

Boil 8 to 10 minutes, or until pasta reaches desired degree of doneness.

Drain in colander.

Remove meat from gravy; place on a serving dish.

Add pasta to gravy; stir; simmer over low heat 5 minutes.

Serve pasta with the meat and a sprinkling of cheese if desired.

SUMMER

Waw-dee-mell-OWN, Tutti Frutti, and the Ladies from the Block

"Watermelon—it's a good fruit. You eat, you drink, you wash your face."
—ENRICO CARUSO

And you can't get enough of it on scaldingly hot Brooklyn summer nights. They are the nights when fire escapes become bedrooms. Living room floors covered with cool white sheets become campgrounds. Tenement roofs become beaches. And streets become playgrounds, ball fields, banquet halls, and multipurpose family rooms, with embossed manhole covers standing in for area rugs.

The watermelon. It's served on the sidewalk from a bowl set atop a rickety bridge table with two legs in the gutter, resting half on and half off the curb. The servers, the daughters of Concetta, Aniella, Maddelana, and Giuseppina, are watched over by their mothers. The older women place their folding chairs at the curb—the better to catch a bit of a breeze.

The children wear jeans or shorts, shirts, and sneakers. The moms wear sundresses and sandals. The nonnas wear cotton housedresses covered by printed cotton "front aprons," beige lisle stockings, tightly laced orthopedic oxfords, and printed cotton kerchiefs to hold their permed hair in place.

The presence of the watermelon on the table begins with its purchase several hours earlier. That's when the brawny young man with the horse-drawn wagon begins his serenade. "Waw-dee-mell-OWN," he sings under the open windows of the tenements along the avenue. And a not-to-be-believed rush takes place before he can sing out, "*Tutti frutti.*"

Yes, he has *tutti frutti*—plums, white peaches, strawberries, and, of course, watermelon. He also has an eye for the ladies. (Lady: the address used by every child at every avenue intersection as in, "Lady, will you cross me?")

And the ladies have an eye for him. A simple purchase of four peaches and a watermelon can take a particularly lucky lady three, four, five minutes. Aniella's daughter, while buying the watermelon that afternoon, bats her eyelashes; he lowers his gaze; she smiles sweetly; he responds in kind.

Aniella calls from an open window, "Don't forget to buy lemons." The spell is broken. With that, her daughter hands over her coins and moves on. And so it goes, until the last lady has smiled on him. As he leads the horse to the next block, he cries out, "Waw-dee-mell-OWN!" In seconds, a line of ladies forms.

Now the watermelon, surrounded by chipped ice, rests in its bowl until each mom wraps a slice in waxed paper and hands it to her child. In the meantime, from their vantage point, the nonnas watch every game going on in the street.

Giuseppina, a cigarette between her lips, calls out warnings, curses, and blessings, depending on whether or not her grandson playing stickball gets a hit, walks, or strikes out. Maddelana clucks her tongue when her granddaughter skins her knee playing potsy. And Concetta leads them in graciously declining an offer of a slice of watermelon. "I'm full; I just ate," each says.

To Concetta, Maddelana, Giuseppina, and Aniella, food is a guilty pleasure—not really something to be enjoyed—unless they're preparing it for a family. Even then, they stab at forkfuls while carrying the serving dish to the table. In a mad ballet, they consume an entire dinner—without ever sitting down.

So as soon as the moms are occupied chatting with one another, Maddelana rises, motions to her compatriots, and begins handing out slices

of watermelon. They make sure to daintily wipe their mouths before the ladies begin to pay attention to them again.

The games end; the children sit and sprawl on the curb, enjoying a last slice of watermelon. The nonnas fold up their chairs. As they carry them away, they turn to one another and nod. And with a saucy wink, Giuseppina reminds Aniella's daughter, "Enjoy buying more watermelon tomorrow."

WATERMELON GRANITA

Serves four

$\frac{2}{3}$ **cup sugar**
$\frac{1}{3}$ **cup water**
Pinch of salt
2 tablespoons lemon juice
1 teaspoon grated lemon rind

1 teaspoon grated orange rind (optional)
4 cups watermelon, diced and seeded

Over medium heat, boil water and sugar together about 5 minutes, or until it becomes syrupy but remains clear; allow to cool.

In a food processor or blender, gently puree watermelon just until pulpy.

Stir sugar syrup and remaining ingredients into watermelon puree.

Freeze mixture in a shallow bowl 2 hours.

Remove from freezer; stir mixture with a fork, breaking up ice granules; return to freezer for 2 hours; stir again, and serve.

Fire Hydrant Days

When the temperature hits the mid-nineties and the linoleum on their kitchen floors starts to buckle, Concetta, Maddelana, Aniella, and Giuseppina realize that even they can't stand the heat in the kitchen. Each carries a folding chair as she leaves her apartment. They set the chairs near the curb. To cool themselves even further, each has rolled her beige lisle stockings down to her ankles. But their black oxfords remain firmly tied.

As if at a given signal, each reaches into the pocket of her front apron and removes a crochet hook, a white linen handkerchief, and a spool of pearly white cotton thread. They nimbly wrap the thread around their left index finger, push the hook through the fabric to pick up a loop, and begin to stitch a lace edge on the hanky.

The grandchildren languish on the stoop; it's too hot for a game of catch. Their mothers are still upstairs cleaning up from dinner—a cooling dish of chicken with salad for a hot night. The jingling bells of an ice cream truck rouse the children. Mothers pop their heads out of windows and toss coins to the children for ice cream.

As the children line up to make a purchase, Concetta warns her granddaughter. "Don't buy the one with the nuts," she says. "You know what nuts do to your stomach."

Maddelana admonishes her grandson, "Careful, don't dirty your shirt." The children, ice cream dripping over their knuckles, return to the stoop. Not a word can be heard.

Approaching footsteps break the silence. Five towering teenagers, one carrying a large wrench, stop in front of a fire hydrant a few feet from the nonnas' chairs.

Aniella is the first to speak up. "What are you doing down here?" she asks.

"You don't belong here," Giuseppina says. "You go to the church up the hill."

A sixth teenager dashes down the stoop. He nods to the guys. "My nonna giving you guys a hard time?" he asks, smiling.

Concetta realizes the new arrival is her grandson. She is so flustered a loop of lace falls from the crochet hook. "You know these boys?" she asks.

"Sure, Nonna, I go to school with them."

"From the other parish?" She has to reassure herself. Is it possible the boys from the, um . . . Irish . . . oh, *other* parish are friends with her grandson? She starts looping thread around her finger. "You go up there too?"

"Nonna, we go to school together; we play ball together. Tonight we're doing something for the kids."

The fellow with the wrench loosens the bolt on the fire hydrant. Water rushes out as the kids rush off the stoop. Their tossed sneakers, shirts, and socks form a path straight to the curb where the children hop into the ankle-deep water. The teenagers press their hands against the open hydrant and create a spray for the gleeful kids.

By now the mothers have joined the nonnas. They encourage the kids to "get good and wet."

Amid the laughter, running, and splashing, Concetta's daughter notices something. She nudges a woman standing next to her and points to Aniella, who is removing her shoes. Aniella nods to the others. Off come the oxfords; off come the lisle stockings. Into the rushing water go the nonnas' feet, unfettered. Ah, bliss.

CHICKEN MILANESE

Serves four

8 chicken cutlets, thinly sliced
$\frac{1}{4}$ cup plus 1 tablespoon olive oil
$\frac{1}{8}$ teaspoon salt
1 $\frac{1}{2}$ cups fresh breadcrumbs, toasted

Preheat oven to 425 degrees F.

Place rimmed sheet pan in oven.

In a shallow bowl, mix $\frac{1}{4}$ cup olive oil with salt; turn cutlets in oil and salt mixture until thoroughly coated.

Sprinkle breadcrumbs on flat plate; dip chicken in crumbs to coat.

Carefully remove hot baking sheet from oven; brush with remaining olive oil. Place cutlets on baking sheet; do not crowd.

Sprinkle cutlets with remaining dipping oil.

Bake 12 to 14 minutes, or until golden brown.

Serve hot, warm, cold, or at room temperature, topped with salad.

SALAD

Serves four

1 head romaine, outer leaves removed, well washed and dried
1 small bunch arugula, stems removed, well washed and dried
1 pint grape tomatoes, halved
1 scallion, well washed, diced
Salt and freshly ground pepper
4 tablespoons olive oil
1 tablespoon lemon juice
$\frac{1}{4}$ cup Gorgonzola in chunks (optional)
3 tablespoons Parmigiano Reggiano in shards (optional)

Tear romaine into bite size pieces.

In a large salad bowl, combine all ingredients, except cheese.

Toss salad; top with Gorgonzola or Parmigiano if desired.

Spoon salad atop each portion of chicken.

Sand in Their Shoes

Coney Island—the boardwalk mecca—at the last stop of the Sea Beach Express. Concetta and Maddelana huff and puff and quietly call out to the saints as they drag grandchildren, ages two to nine, across the platform and down the subway stairs. Thus begins a day of fun in the sun in Brooklyn, 1947.

The children are wearing shorts—bathing suits underneath—and the wicker of the subway seats has embossed the backs of their thighs with a cross-hatch pattern. Concetta and Maddelana, too, are ready for the beach. They wear housedresses, seamed stockings rolled beneath their knees, black oxfords, and, in deference to the 89-degree temperature, no front aprons.

Concetta and Maddelana push the children along the boardwalk to keep them from making eye contact with vendors selling corn on the cob, hot dogs, and cotton candy, and to avoid barkers touting skeet-ball games where players can win "a glass candy dish."

The children barely take the first step off the boardwalk before they start complaining. "The sand is too hot; the sand's in my shoes," and on they go. Concetta soothes them and ends up carrying the youngest one across the sand. They pick a spot that's perfect for dashing into the ocean. "This is a good spot," Maddelana says. "Far enough away from the boardwalk so the children won't see what goes on under there."

Blanket spread out, towels pulled from shopping bags, coconut-scented suntan lotion applied, the children, except for the baby, head for the water. Maddelana, a sentry, stands guard at the water's edge. She doesn't know how to swim; she wears her oxfords; and she holds a two-year-old. But her eyes never leave the children playing a foot away from her. And if she suspects danger, her voice can carry over the waves all the way to the coast of Maine. Every few minutes, she bends down, cups some water in her hand, and spreads it over the baby's face, hands, and neck, secretly pleased when some drops fall on her now too-hot housedress.

It's time for the changing of the guard. Concetta, shoes on, approaches Maddelana, takes the baby in her arms, and repeats the saltwater almost-baptismal ritual.

The children, lively and hungry, return to the blanket. They want to eat quickly so they can begin to observe the Brooklyn rule: no swimming until an hour after eating. From their shopping bags, Concetta and Maddelana take a thermos of lemonade and a brown paper bag filled with sandwiches.

Concetta and Maddelana have been in this war together: herding children, applying their suntan lotion, and watching them swim. Concetta would have given her life for Maddelana's grandchild, as Maddelana would for hers. But now they are enemies. The battlefield—the blanket. The spoils —the lunch sandwiches.

"What did you bring today?" Concetta asks

"Frittata sandwiches," Maddelana answers. "How about you?"

"I made peanut butter and jelly on American bread."

Maddelana raises her eyebrows as if to ask, "What kind of sandwich is that?"

A detente is reached as they watch the children, with lips still salty from a frittata feast, devour PB&Js.

Contentedly, Concetta lies on the blanket. "I think I take a little rest now," she says.

POTATO FRITTATA

Makes six sandwiches

$\frac{1}{4}$ **cup olive oil**
4 baking potatoes, well-scrubbed, thinly sliced, dried
Salt to taste
8 large eggs, beaten just to blend
Pinch of salt
6 Italian or Sicilian round rolls

Preheat broiler.

In an ovenproof skillet, heat olive oil.

Gently place potatoes in oil; reduce heat to medium; toss potatoes with a spatula; fry until golden and tender; sprinkle with salt.

Beat eggs with a pinch of salt; pour eggs over potatoes; rotating pan so eggs cover all.

Lift edges of omelet as eggs cook so raw eggs flow to bottom of pan.

When omelet is almost set; place under broiler for about 4 minutes; watch carefully; broil until golden brown and puffed.

Serve warm or at room temperature as a main dish, or slice omelet into six pieces and fill rolls.

Fireworks

Concetta, Maddelana, Aniella, and Giuseppina don't drive. (For that matter, neither do their husbands.) Instead they rely on sons, sons-in-law, sons of *cumare* (godmothers), and sons of neighbors to get them where they have to go. And they do go—primarily to visit the grave of the most recently buried relative or a daughter who moved to Nassau (the county, not the island), or to a shrine, a monastery, or a cathedral.

Every so often though, on a summer Tuesday night, Concetta, Aniella, and Maddelana do not have to ask for a ride. One of the available drivers invites them to tool down Stillwell Avenue at Coney Island and see the fireworks. They are expected to be ready for their ride by 7:30. But they are often late. Getting food ready for the journey (even though they served dinner at six o'clock), gathering the grandchildren, taking off their front aprons—these things take time.

Concetta calls out a window to extend an invitation to any grandchild playing nearby. "Come on," she says. "We're going to the fireworks."

Numbers do not concern her. One lap can hold two grandchildren and often does. Thus, there are Concetta and Maddelana and four grandchildren in the backseat, Aniella and one grandchild in the passenger seat, and the driver, a total of nine making their way out of the neighborhood.

On the drive, the kids tease, insult, and abuse one another. Concetta alternates between yelling at the children and looking out the window to grin at and wave to neighbors who do not have the luck to get to the big show. After a while, to calm the kids, Aniella reaches into her brown lunch bag and pulls out shoestrings of licorice. (A *cumari* who works in a candy factory provides the somewhat misshapen samples free of charge.) Because each child has the same sweet, there is no haggling.

The driver parks the car as close as he can to the boardwalk. The children pile out, waiting a few minutes for the auto to get cool before they climb on the hood, the fenders, and the roof—their perfect viewing spots. The nonnas surround the vehicle. It's nighttime, and they are responsible for the children. Aniella says, "Who knows what can happen in the dark."

Concetta and Maddelana shake their heads solemnly. "Besides, we have to stay nearby to make sure they eat," Maddelana says. Relieved, they nod and smile.

The first whiff of gunpowder tickles their noses, and the children become silent. They even stop punching one another and making devil's horns atop their buddies' heads. And Concetta, Maddelana, and Aniella, to make sure they don't enjoy the colorful spectacle too much, busy themselves with handing out sandwiches filled with their dinners' leftovers.

A nonna doesn't worry about what kind of sandwich she gives the kids: peppers and eggs, meatballs, veal parmigiana—all good. What matters to her—although she's determined not to show it—is the way the driver is going to respond to her offering. The driver accepts and polishes off a sandwich from each nonna. They bring him cookies, licorice, and a thermos of espresso laced with a drop of anisette. And they wait.

"Thanks" he says, casually. "That was some snack."

Concetta, Maddelana, and Aniella look deflated as they start to munch on whatever remains in their lunch bags.

VEAL PARMIGIANA

Serves six

2 large eggs, well beaten
1½ cups fresh bread crumbs
Salt
Freshly ground black pepper
2 pounds thin veal cutlets
¼ cup olive oil
1 pound whole milk mozzarella, thinly sliced
2 cups tomato sauce, homemade or store-bought
3 tablespoons fresh basil, finely minced, or 1 teaspoon dried
2 tablespoons grated Parmigiano Reggiano (optional)

Preheat oven to 375 degrees F.

Add salt and pepper to eggs; dip cutlets in egg mixture, then in bread crumbs.

In large skillet, heat oil over medium heat; sauté cutlets a few at a time in oil.

Add five tablespoons sauce to a nonreactive shallow casserole.

Add a layer of veal, a sprinkle of basil, a layer of mozzarella, and a sprinkle of tomato sauce; continue layering ingredients; ending with a layer of mozzarella.

Sprinkle with a few tablespoons of sauce; add Parmigiano if you like.

Bake 30 minutes, or until top layer is bubbling and golden.

Let rest 10 minutes at room temperature before serving.

How the Garden Grows

Zucchini, zucchini, zucchini everywhere! Light green, dark green, striped, yellow with orange-tinged ends. Some weigh two pounds, some weigh four; a few weigh four ounces and a tiny bit more. The nonnas' front aprons are too small to carry the vegetables from yard to apartment.

Lugging a bushel basket, Aniella arrives at her zucchini patch. She picks, cuts, and pulls to rid her garden of the glistening gems that are strangling every other plant in sight. In minutes, the basket is full.

She finishes harvesting and gathers with Maddelana and Giuseppina on a front stoop to talk about—what else?—zucchini. "Peel them first, then make whatever you want with them," says Aniella.

As soon as Maddelana hears the word "peel," she shakes her head wildly; her eyes widen, and her hands make dismissive gestures even before she opens her mouth. "What is this *peel*?" she asks. "All you got to do is use a vegetable brush and scrub them under running water."

"No," insists Giuseppina. "When you leave the peel on, they taste bitter." Maddelana says, "They're not bitter if you salt them first and leave them in a colander to drain."

"Who's got that kind of time?" asks Aniella. "Besides they're so fresh, they won't be bitter."

The zucchini talk stops when their grandchildren, as if at a given signal, come out to play. But no games can begin until the nonnas have pinched the children's cheeks. All the nonnas pinch the cheeks of all the kids. Aniella, pinching her own grandchild, swiftly reaches into the pocket of her front apron and pulls out a dime. She whispers to the child, "For later, you buy an ice cream."

So absorbed is each nonna in this same subterfuge, not one realizes that the others are also whispering and distributing coins to their own grandchildren. The boys and girls dash off, and each nonna is content, believing she has a secret.

Now it's the thwack of a Spaldeen the kids toss against a brick building that punctuates the conversation about zucchini.

"I'm making zucchini cakes tonight," Maddelana says. "I'll fry them in a little olive oil. I should go and chop the zucchini soon."

"*Chop* the zucchini? Giuseppina asks, aghast. "You use the cheese grater to make nice smooth shreds. Then you make the pancakes."

"The only way to get the zucchini cakes right is to use a potato peeler and make strips, then chop the strips," says Maddelana.

"I'm not chopping, grating, or making strips because I'm making stuffed zucchini," says Aniella.

"So will you peel them or scrub them?" asks Giuseppina. And so it goes.

STUFFED ZUCCHINI

Serves four

5 medium-size zucchini, well-scrubbed, halved lengthwise
6 tablespoons olive oil
1 medium-size onion, diced
3 slices white bread, in 1-inch cubes
¼ cup vermouth or dry white wine
Salt and pepper to taste
¼ cup Parmigiano Reggiano, coarsely grated

Preheat oven to 400 degrees F.

Steam zucchini halves for 5 minutes in lightly salted water to cover; remove to paper towels to drain.

Use a teaspoon to remove the flesh from the inside of each zucchini, leaving a shell of about $\frac{1}{2}$ inch; set shells aside; dice flesh; set aside.

In 4 tablespoons olive oil, sauté onion until golden; sprinkle with salt and pepper.

Add diced zucchini and cubed bread; sauté mixture until bread is golden; add vermouth; reduce over medium heat.

Spread a tablespoon of remaining olive oil in a nonreactive 9 x 12-inch casserole.

Stuff zucchini shells with filling; place halves in pan; sprinkle with cheese and remaining olive oil.

Bake 25 to 30 minutes, or until bubbling and golden on top.

The War of the Flowers

Early on midsummer mornings, Concetta, Maddelana, and Aniella descend to tend their backyard gardens. Each of their separate little plots is surrounded by a very short wooden picket fence.

They hurry because squash blossoms are in bloom. To get the maximum flavor and freshness out of the short-season flowers, the nonnas must pick them as soon as they open, wash them, prepare them, and serve them the same evening. And gathering the flowers in their front aprons, instead of a basket or bowl, assures them that they are babying the blossoms.

As Concetta plucks each open bud, she keeps an eye on Aniella, who is picking blossoms in her own little spot. The morning progresses, and the results of the bounty caught in an apron turns into a contest. Bragging rights fall into three categories: who has picked the most, whose flowers are the largest, and—prize of prizes—whose flowers have a glorious teeny, tiny green zucchini attached to the bloom.

The serious work of cleaning the flowers begins as Concetta enters her apartment, places the flowers in a pristine kitchen sink, and begins to douse each with super cold water—so cold she has to wipe her reddened hands on a towel every few minutes. She wraps the flowers in kitchen towels and refrigerates them, dries her hands, and steps outdoors.

She joins Maddelana and Aniella as they set up their folding chairs near the curb. After greeting one another, they get around to the morning's significant results.

Concetta says offhandedly, "I picked, oh, about a dozen, and they were big—perfect for stuffing."

"You know," says Aniella, "if they're too big, they're bitter."

"The eight I picked are medium-size, but one has a tiny zucchini attached," Maddelana says. She sighs contentedly and crosses her hands in the bib of her front apron. "The tiny one is so cute."

"I didn't have much luck today," says Giuseppina approaching. The others cluck sympathetically and fight the urge to grin. "I picked nine, very small; maybe I should have left them for tomorrow."

"Well, you can't stuff them," says Concetta, sounding satisfied.

"No, but I can put them in the frittata I'm serving tonight when Father Angelo comes to dinner."

The clout of the clergy visiting for dinner silences them. Finally Aniella asks, "Did you listen to Jack Benny on Sunday night?"

All talk of zucchini blossoms is ended for the day. Giuseppina smiles gently. Defying all the odds, she has won the contest.

STUFFED ZUCCHINI BLOSSOMS

Serves six

18 to 20 zucchini blossoms, washed, stems and core removed,
   thoroughly dried
2 pounds whole milk ricotta
1 pound whole milk mozzarella, diced
1 large egg, well beaten
Salt
Freshly ground pepper
2 tablespoons flat-leaf parsley, minced
Zucchini attached to blossom, finely diced (optional)
$\frac{1}{2}$ to $\frac{3}{4}$ cup olive oil

In a large bowl, make the filling; mix together all ingredients, except blossoms, and olive oil.

Stuff each blossom generously with filling.

Heat a large, broad skillet over medium heat; add $\frac{1}{2}$ cup olive oil.

Gently lower a few blossoms at a time into the hot oil; do not crowd the pan; add additional oil if needed for frying a second batch.

Sauté blossoms about 5 minutes on each side, turning carefully.

Remove blossoms to platter lined with paper towels; sprinkle with additional salt; serve.

ZUCCHINI BLOSSOM FRITTATA

Serves four

6 to 9 zucchini blossoms, washed, stems and core removed, thoroughly dried, sliced into strips
2 tablespoons shallots, minced
Salt
Freshly ground pepper to taste
8 eggs, beaten
Pinch of salt
¼ cup olive oil
6 tablespoons Parmigiano Reggiano, coarsely grated

Preheat broiler.

Heat a large, broad skillet over medium heat; add olive oil.

Gently lower the blossoms into the hot oil; sauté blossoms about 3 minutes.

Stir in shallots; sauté blossom-shallot mixture until shallots brown slightly.

Sprinkle with salt and pepper.

Add pinch of salt to beaten eggs; pour eggs over zucchini mixture; reduce heat to low.

Use a heatproof rubber spatula to work eggs away from the side of the pan.

When edges of the omelet turn golden, sprinkle cheese over it.

Place skillet about 5 inches under broiler for about 4 minutes; watch carefully.

When cheese is melted and golden and omelet is cooked through, remove to serving platter.

The Name Game

A new baby on the block! A new baby on the block! Concetta, Aniella, Maddelana, and Giuseppina are all excited. Mother and child won't leave the hospital for several days, but the nonnas have their arsenal of new-baby regalia ready.

"I knitted some booties and caps," Giuseppina says. "My hands are still sore." As usual, she brings the others up to date on her aches and pains.

Concetta ignores her complaint and starts talking about "beautiful pillowcases I embroidered—fit for a prince!"

"I made a little kimono with tiny red ribbons on it," Aniella says. "To keep away the *mal'occhio*."

"Oof, I was so busy with church, I didn't have time to make anything, so I bought a bunch of fruit and some pasta for a gift and a box of regina, the cookies sprinkled with sesame seeds," Maddelana says.

They sit on the stoop, stringing and tipping the big, flat, green Romano beans that fill their front aprons. Early in the morning, all but one had made marinara sauce to coat the beans as they simmer. Concetta announces that she is cooking the beans "in a new way, with a smoked ham hock." The others raise their eyebrows and continue to exchange remarks about "the crispness, the color, the juiciness"—they find many things to say about beans.

When they finish stringing and tipping, they tie the beans, the loose tips, and the curly strings into their aprons. They rise as though ready to step inside, when Aniella asks "What's she going to name the baby?"

"Three daughters, now a son," says Concetta. "You know she named the first girl after her mother-in-law."

"That's the custom; it's only right," Giuseppina says.

"Yes, but since the second one was also a girl, she named her Louise. That is after her father-in-law, Louis," Maddelana says, shaking her head.

"She should name the boy for her father-in-law anyway," Aniella says, shaking her head.

"Now she named the third girl the right way—after her mother," Concetta says.

"So what will she call this boy?" Maddelana asks.

"She can't name him after her own father," Giuseppina says firmly. "That shows disrespect for her father-in-law—the first boy and all."

"I wouldn't like to be in her shoes," Concetta says.

Several days later, mother and baby come home. As the mother cradles the swaddled infant, she makes her way up the stoop, and the nonnas extend their good wishes. They hand the gifts to the dad, who is following the mother.

Concetta cries, "So beautiful."

"He's perfect," Aniella says, pulling back the blanket covering the baby's face. Each makes a sign of the cross on the infant's forehead.

Concetta hesitates. Finally, she asks, "What did you name the baby?"

"We named him Peter Mario. Peter for my husband, and Mario after me—Maria."

The nonnas breathe a sigh of relief. The name doesn't follow the naming tradition. But who can blame a father for calling a son after himself, they all agree. Another family crisis averted.

ROMANO BEANS IN SAUCE

Serves four

1 onion, finely diced
1 clove garlic quartered
3 tablespoons olive oil
Salt
Freshly ground pepper
1 bay leaf
Sprinkle dried oregano
3 cups tomato sauce, homemade or store-bought
2 pounds Romano beans, washed, tipped, strings removed

In a heavy nonreactive pan over medium heat, sauté all ingredients except tomato sauce and beans.

When onion and garlic are golden, add tomato sauce.

Simmer 20 minutes, or until sauce thickens.

Add beans, cover partially, simmer over low heat 30 to 40 minutes, or until beans are fork-tender; serve.

ROMANO BEANS WITH HAM

Serves four

3 quarts cold water
Two 2-pound smoked ham hocks, washed
1 bay leaf
$\frac{1}{4}$ teaspoon whole peppercorns
$\frac{1}{4}$ teaspoon dried thyme
2 pounds Romano beans, washed, tipped, strings removed

Place all ingredients, except beans, in a 4-quart nonreactive pot.

Over high heat, bring to a boil.

Skim froth from surface.

Reduce heat to medium.

Simmer 2 hours, or until meat is falling off the bone.

Remove ham hocks; return skin and bones to pot; dice meat, set aside.

Add beans to simmering liquid in pot; simmer 30 to 40 minutes, or until beans are fork-tender.

With slotted spoon, remove beans from pot; discard skin and bones.

Add diced meat to beans; serve.

A Block Party

It's easy to organize a guest list for a party when all the invitees live within a three-block radius, and some—like Concetta, Maddelana, and Aniella— live in apartments in the same building. So for any occasion worth cele- brating—a baptism, a First Communion, a cousin arriving from the old country—the number of people invited to a party held on a sidewalk and spilling over into a street is enormous. No apartment is large enough to hold all the nonnas, nonnos, *zias*, *zios*, *sorelli*, and *fratelli*, and, of course, the parish priests.

Heaven defend the host who neglects to invite a family member or neighbor. Besides losing the affection and respect of the non-invitee, the host stands to lose half the guests. "You don't invite my niece Maria, I don't come," Concetta says threateningly as she approaches the host of an upcoming party.

So the block party is born. No invitations needed. If a nonna can see the festivities as she looks out a window, she is invited. No decorations needed— only the starched and ironed tablecloths on card tables surrounded by folding chairs. No hard liquor needed. A keg of beer resting on two wooden saw horses, jugs of wine, and sodas resting on ice in washtubs are the beverages of choice. No band needed. A nonno with an accordion and a friend with a mandolin are the music-makers.

The party begins at 5pm and lasts until . . . .

Little children run underfoot. Giuseppina holds the baptismal baby for a second, pinching the baby's cheek before passing the baby to Aniella. Concetta and Maddelana are in the middle of the street, linking arms and clapping their hands over their heads while dancing a tarantella.

As the music ends, Concetta says, "Come on, we have to help put out the hot dishes."

She and Maddelana move carefully through the crowd as they carry hot dishes from a main serving table to the guests' tables. "Watch out," Maddelana says to the children.

"Oh, these kids," Aniella says, exasperated. "They don't know everyone is waiting for the food." Guests sit at each table for only a minute—just long enough to taste the special dish there—and then move on to the next table.

All is fun and frivolity as dessert time approaches. Concetta, Aniella, and Maddelana have volunteered to make sweets for the party. Giuseppina prefers to be a guest. "I'll just sit here," she says. "I didn't bake, but I got the baby a nice gift." Maddelana raises her eyebrows at her sister. Giuseppina, too busy smoking, doesn't even notice Maddelana's annoyance.

Concetta rises from the table with a good deal of fussing and throat clearing as she announces to the neighbors sitting on either side what her mission is. "I'm going to get the sweets now—the ones I made myself. You," she enlists preteen boys, "come and help me with the carrying."

Now Maddelana and Aniella join Concetta to form a procession leading the blushing boys from table to table distributing the cakes and pastries. Each nonna has prepared her specialty, and the tension is strong as each attempts to overhear rave reviews of her dish.

The guests are talking about baseball, the baby's sleeping habits, the price of sausage, the newest pizzeria. But nobody mentions the sweets. As the nonnas wend their way back up the street, they notice that each table holds empty dessert dishes. The guests have consumed every generous morsel in the time it took for the nonnas and their crew to serve them.

Concetta, Maddelana, and Aniella sit down at Giuseppina's table. "Next party, I only make pasta," Concetta says. "That's easy, not like the cream puffs."

"Next party, I'm not even going," says Maddelana, as she dismisses the whole affair by dusting her hands together.

"This time, I have no choice; it's my neighbor's granddaughter's baptism," Aniella says. "But next party, I invite you all to go to the movies with me. Maybe we'll see something good with Esther Williams in it."

"Bah!" Giuseppina says. "Just do what I do. Bring a nice gift."

....

CREAM PUFFS

Makes 24 party-size puffs

1 cup water
½ cup (1 stick) unsalted butter
1 teaspoon sugar
½ teaspoon salt
1 cup unbleached all-purpose flour
4 large eggs, room temperature

Preheat oven to 450 degrees F.

Bring water, butter, sugar, and salt to a boil.

Add flour all at once; stir flour into water mixture until a thick paste forms and the batter leaves the sides of the pan.

Place batter into bowl of electric mixer.

With flat beater, beat eggs into batter one at a time until the batter is smooth and glossy.

Drop batter by rounded teaspoons on a buttered baking sheet.

Bake 12 minutes; reduce oven temperature to 350 degrees F, and bake 25 to 30 minutes, or until puffs are golden; cool puffs on wire rack.

WHIPPED CREAM FILLING

2 cups heavy cream
3 tablespoons sugar
$\frac{1}{4}$ teaspoon vanilla extract
1 cup confectioners' sugar

Chill beater and bowl in freezer.

Add cream, granulated sugar, and vanilla extract to cold bowl; whip until cream is light and fluffy.

Slice each puff in half horizontally; fill with cream mixture; use a small strainer to dust confectioners' sugar over tops of the filled puffs.

....

RICOTTA CREAM FILLING

2 cups whole milk ricotta, drained
5 tablespoons plus 1 cup confectioners' sugar
Grated rind of 1 orange
$\frac{1}{4}$ teaspoon vanilla extract

Beat together ricotta, 5 tablespoons confectioners' sugar, orange rind, and vanilla until creamy.

Slice each puff in half horizontally; fill with cream mixture; use a small strainer to dust the 1 cup confectioners' sugar over tops of the filled puffs.

Guarding the Fireside

There are no flowery fields of clover in Brooklyn. So on hot summer nights, streets and sidewalks become family rooms, and tiny backyards become campgrounds.

The grandsons gather their supplies for their campfire feast—Aniella provides a rickety four-legged metal burner that should hold a can of Sterno; Giuseppina carries a bunch of twigs and newspapers to place on the burner; Maddelana donates a can opener and a bottle opener. Concetta is in charge of the feast. She presents new potatoes that she has scrubbed to a pristine state, as many cans of Heinz Pork and Beans as there are guests, and bottles of Mission soda—grape, cream, lemon-lime.

The boys set up camp as far away as they can from both the circle of folding chairs the nonnas occupy and the fig tree. About the fig tree? Giuseppina has warned them to within an inch of their lives, waving her cigarette all the while for emphasis, to keep their distance. Aniella shoos away the campgoers' younger siblings, especially sisters, as soon as they step foot in the yard.

The boys each throw a flaming Diamond wooden match to ignite the crumpled newspapers the twigs rest on. Their mothers lean out of second-story and third-story windows or sit on fire escapes watching the dinner party. Even though they find the boys and their fire-making activity nerve-wracking and it gives them occasion to bite their fingers in frustration, they respond to the nonnas' leave-them-alone hand motions and suffer in silence.

In the nonnas' circle it's outdoor crochet season—and their fingertips dance nimbly to create lace doilies from fine ecru thread.

The embers are glowing brightly as the boys toss the potatoes into the makeshift oven. The crisp click of a can opener piercing a can is followed by the release of the sticky sweet scent of pork and beans. Each boy places his newly opened main course alongside the fire that holds the potatoes.

"Bah, the spoons, the spoons," Maddelana says. "They forgot the spoons." She rises and goes into the building. In the meantime, Aniella and Concetta call upon all the saints in heaven to protect the boys from setting their hair on fire. Giuseppina is about to do the same as she lights a Chesterfield.

The boys have commandeered an old tin tray from a local bar to use as a serving dish for the potatoes. Chipped white soup bowls on loan from Maddelana's kitchen will hold the beans. Anticipation fills the air as the boys use tongs to push and pull spuds out of the fire and pour the barely lukewarm beans into the bowls. Maddelana passes out the spoons.

The boys are about to dig in. But the oldest in the group signals to the others to gather around. Each boy begins to spoon a portion of beans and broken bits of potato into a bowl. They throw out their fingers in "once, twice, three, SHOOT!" to choose a bowl carrier. The chore, or the honor, falls to one of the youngest.

As he walks across the yard, he carefully balances the bowl that now holds four spoons in addition to the food. He presents the offering to Concetta and says, "You each have a spoon."

Surprised and pleased, but never expressing too much (or any) praise, each thanks the boys in her own way. "Thank you," Aniella says. "But you're lucky you didn't burn your eyelashes off."

"This is very good," Giuseppina says, savoring a mouthful. "It has a nice smoky taste."

"Thank you," Maddelana says, "and thank heaven your mother didn't see you almost catch your shirt on fire."

"Thanks," Concetta says. "This looks really good, but did you remember to rinse the top of the can before you opened the beans?"

The dish-bearer starts running to his buddies—all the while, shaking his head and waving his arms in disbelief.

BAKED PORK AND BEANS

Serves eight

1 pound dry navy beans
1 bay leaf
Dash salt
Freshly ground pepper
$\frac{3}{4}$ pound double-smoked bacon
1 onion, sliced into thin rounds
$\frac{1}{2}$ cup molasses
$\frac{1}{2}$ cup brown sugar
4 teaspoons dry mustard
4 tablespoons catsup
5 whole cloves
1 large sprig fresh thyme, or $\frac{1}{2}$ teaspoon dried

Rinse beans; soak in a nonreactive casserole overnight.

Drain soaked beans; add cold water to cover beans by 3 inches; add bay leaf, dash of salt and pepper; bring to boil.

Reduce heat; cover casserole; simmer beans $1\frac{1}{2}$ to 2 hours, or until tender; drain beans well.

Preheat oven to 250 degrees F.

Remove rind from bacon; dice bacon into $\frac{3}{4}$-inch cubes; blanch bacon and rind in boiling water 10 minutes; drain; rinse.

To the casserole, add a layer of beans, a layer of onions, and a layer of bacon; repeat layering, ending with a layer of bacon and the rind on top.

Mix remaining ingredients together; pour over beans in casserole; add enough boiling water to cover the beans by 1 inch.

Check throughout cooking time; add more boiling water if necessary.

Bake 5 to 6 hours, or until beans have absorbed most of the liquid.

Uncover casserole for last half hour of baking.

My Town's Better Than Your Town

The young mothers—or ladies on the block—get together every weekday to pick up the children from school and on Sundays to go to Mass as a family. They trade recipes, make suggestions for getting the most out of their treadle sewing machines, and plan a schedule to bring dishes to a new mother. No conflict, then, exists between those ladies whose families came from Naples, Calabria, Abruzzi—or even Sicily.

The nonnas, though, never forget where they came from, and they often find it difficult to be gracious toward those who arrived from another province, never mind a separate island. And the former island-dwellers will often stick it to the former mainlanders by slipping in a word or two in their Sicilian dialect when conversing with them. This causes the mainlanders to be on their toes in all meetings with the islanders.

But the groups coexist peacefully enough at neighborhood weddings, church gatherings, and, of course, funerals. A death in the neighborhood brings the opportunity to earn a thousand friendship points. The nonnas can present a generous donation in an envelope at the wake, offer enough money to the priest to have an "announced" Mass said for the deceased, or prepare a meal for the family.

So cordiality often reigns among the dissonant factions, until the ladies bring them together in a situation that emphasizes their differences. Take, for example, Aniella's and Concetta's families renting vacation cabins next door to each other. Aniella is Sicilian, Concetta Neapolitan. The two are good friends, agreeing on all food-related matters.

For Concetta and Aniella, the highlight of a week in the country is the opportunity it gives them to pull more weeds than they could in their city gardens. And if a nonna meets a nonna while hanging swimsuits out to dry, their conversation is about—food.

"What are you making for dinner?" Concetta asks.

"Caponata," says Aniella.

Ah! A Sicilian dish that's prepared by mainlanders too.

"I think I'll do the same," Concetta says. "The eggplant at the farmstand looks very nice."

After dinner, the two families gather around a fire and watch the kids toast marshmallows. It's a pleasant, relaxing occasion until Aniella quietly starts to sing a Sicilian folk song about a donkey, *"Ce una scicaderru . . ."*

From the other side of the fire, in an edgy voice, Concetta starts to sing a Neapolitan song about a donkey, *"E tire, tire, tire i ciucciarella . . ."*

Mothers and kids drowsing by the fire take up the cry. Tales of the two donkeys grow louder and louder. A night in the country, orchestrated by the nonnas.

CAPONATA

Serves eight as an appetizer or side dish

1 one-pound eggplant, unpeeled, diced into $\frac{3}{4}$-inch cubes
1 onion, thinly sliced
1 head fennel, thinly sliced
6 stalks celery, sliced into $\frac{3}{4}$-inch pieces
$\frac{1}{2}$ cup olive oil
Salt
Freshly ground pepper
$\frac{1}{4}$ cup Sicilian olives, pitted, diced
1 tablespoon pine nuts
1 tablespoon tiny capers, rinsed, dried

1 8-ounce can tomato sauce

2 tablespoons red wine vinegar

2 tablespoons sugar, or to taste

In a large nonreactive pan, warm 2 tablespoons oil.

Sauté each vegetable separately, until golden; add more oil as necessary.

Remove each vegetable from the pan when golden; sprinkle with salt and pepper.

Combine the browned vegetables and their juices in the pan; add olives, capers, and pine nuts; stir.

Add tomato sauce; stir; bring to a simmer.

Add vinegar and sugar; stir.

Simmer partially covered 25 to 30 minutes, stirring often, until sauce thickens and vegetables have absorbed the sauce.

Serve at room temperature or chilled.

Hot Stuff

In the backyard, Concetta, Aniella, and Maddelana's front aprons are full, full, full, brimming with hot peppers—long ones, chubby cherry ones, and wrinkly oval ones. Red, green, and striped red and green stems curl around the nonnas' fingers as each picks one more to add to the bunch.

When they return to the stoop after cleaning their crop, each carries a bunch of the longest, reddest peppers, a spool of thick thread, and a huge quilting needle. Concetta threads her needle, knots the end of the double strand, and begins to string peppers one at a time through their green stems. She and the others are stringing the peppers so they can be hung to dry. Giuseppina with only a Chesterfield in her hand, no peppers, joins them on the stoop.

"I hope it's not damp tomorrow so the peppers have a chance to start drying," Maddelana says.

"I hang them and forget them," Aniella says. "I don't even use them until Thanksgiving,"

"The best are the fresh, like the ones we picked today," says Concetta, "fried for a long, long time in oil with garlic and salt."

The others shake their heads when she says "a long, long time."

"No," Maddelana says. "You should cook them for only a few minutes in the oil, add the salt and garlic, and that's it." She weaves the needle through her front apron, freeing her hands to dust them together. As far as she's concerned, the case is closed. But the others disagree.

For once, Giuseppina agrees with her sister. "You're right. That's the way we learned from Mamma, and she made them the best."

But Concetta insists her peppers are better than the best. "I'm making them tonight," she says. "I'll bring you a taste after dinner."

The others raise their eyebrows, look at one another, and avoid looking at her. Who is going to make hot peppers better than the ones they make—fast-fried—the ones their mothers taught them how to make?

On this end-of-summer evening, the men have already moved a card table to the curb for their nightly game of *brisc*. Concetta commandeers the table, moves the deck of cards to the side, and places on the table a bowl of crisp, faceted slices of jewel-like peppers glistening with olive oil and sprinkled with tiny, golden nuggets of garlic. She removes a large loaf of crisp bread from a brown bag and tears the bag open to serve as a tray for the bread.

At the sight—and the scent—of the peppers, the men become the first to help themselves, breaking off bits of bread to scoop up the tasty offering.

Aniella, Maddelana, and Giuseppina saunter to the table and pretend not to hear the men commenting on how delicious the peppers are. Aniella, who dries peppers "until Thanksgiving," is the first to use the bread to sop up a bit of oil and fold it around a few peppers. She licks her lips but remains silent as the others dig in.

When Giuseppina notices that only a few peppers and some shards of bread remain, she eases her way to the table, picks up a crust of bread, and begins vigorously wiping the bowl clean. Then she downs the bread in one gulp. No more will she be fast-frying hot peppers.

Concetta waits for a verdict.

"They're all right," Giuseppina says, "but they could use a little more salt."

SLOW-FRIED HOT PEPPERS

Serves four

1 pound long, green and red Italian hot peppers
3 cloves diced garlic
1 teaspoon salt
¼ cup olive oil

Slice peppers, including seeds, into ¼-inch rounds.

Place all ingredients in a skillet large enough to hold them in
one layer.

Simmer over very low heat 45 minutes to 1 hour, or until peppers
are shiny and crisp and garlic is golden.

SERVING SUGGESTIONS
Spoon on slices of toasted country bread.
Spoon on toasted bread and top with slices of mozzarella.
Stir a few into scrambled eggs.
Spoon over breaded and browned chicken or pork cutlets.
Stir into pasta with chickpeas, peas, or anchovies.
Sprinkle over green salad or tuna salad.
Spoon on a sesame roll and top with provolone.
Stir a few into quick-fried broccoli rabe.

We Need the Eggs

On a hot August afternoon, the nonnas sit on folding chairs at the curb. They crochet lace trim on linen handkerchiefs and watch the children play in water spewing from a fire hydrant.

"Too hot to cook tonight," Maddelana says. "Maybe I make sandwiches."

The others, almost in a chorus, pooh-pooh her. "You know you're going to cook—just make something easy, like eggs," her sister Giuseppina says.

"I have to cook eggs in a new way," Concetta says. "Before the boys went away to The War, they ate only fried eggs, scrambled eggs, and frittata. Now they want eggs easy-over—I don't know—or over-easy, eggs on top of grits with sausage, and sometimes in what they call a Western omelet."

"It's true," Aniella says. "For years I tried to get my son to eat polenta, and it was always, 'You're kidding me, Ma, not that.' Since he comes home, he takes the corn meal out of the cabinet and asks me to make grits. I follow the instructions on the package and fry eggs and sausages to serve with the grits. I take some grits myself. If I add some cheese and a drop of olive oil, I have polenta." She shakes her head. "But he calls it grits."

The tinkling bell of the Bungalow Bar truck coming down the avenue causes a rush of dripping wet children to run to their nonnas for coins. They are eager to buy a toasted almond pop, or a coconut-covered pop, or a traditional pop draped in chocolate.

Concetta's older grandsons hand their unopened ice cream to her and ask permission to take a ride in the Bungalow Bar truck. "All right, you go," she says, "but be careful." Faces beaming, they run past the younger children and climb into the front seat next to the driver. The ride lasts only a few blocks, and the boys step out of the truck when the driver makes the next stop. Then they race each other to pick up their ice cream.

Concetta hands them the pops and issues a warning, "Don't get that stuff all over you. Eat nice."

The nonnas' fingers move swiftly as they crochet. But Giuseppina puts down her crochet hook and lights up a Chesterfield. "It's because they went to those places, you know. Virginia, Kentucky, Tennessee," she says. "That's where they learned about all those different ways to make eggs. When they were overseas, they never even saw an egg."

"Aha," Aniella says, and the others nod in agreement. After indicting all the states beyond New Jersey, Aniella says, "Still it's not so bad to learn something new. . . . How do I make a Western omelet?"

All who know shout out an ingredient or two, adding to those already mentioned. Aniella calls to her grandson. "Here, take this quarter. Go to the store and buy a quarter pound of ham." She dusts her hands together and turns to the others. "I always have peppers in the house."

"So you're going to make it?" Maddelana asks.

"Why not? But maybe I sprinkle it with a little Parmigiano—be tastier that way."

WESTERN OMELET

Serves one

1 tablespoon olive oil
6 tablespoons diced ham or prosciutto
$\frac{1}{2}$ sweet pepper, red or green, seeded, diced
2 tablespoons minced onion
3 large eggs, well beaten
Salt and freshly ground pepper to taste
1 tablespoon Parmigiano Reggiano or Cheddar cheese, grated (optional)

Heat oil in small skillet or omelet pan.

Reduce heat to medium low; add peppers, ham, onions, and salt and pepper to taste.

Sauté until ham crisps, peppers are tender, and onion is translucent.

Pour eggs over all; tilt pan to cover entire surface.

Cook until eggs are set.

Turn omelet over to set second side, about 3 minutes; serve sprinkled with cheese if desired.

A Winery–in Brooklyn?

As Concetta opens the door that separates the vestibule from the main hallway in her tenement apartment, she can smell a fruity but almost acrid odor. She follows her nose to the back of the hallway where the door with the hook and latch leads to the cellar stairs. The smell grows stronger as she descends the rickety, poorly lighted staircase and brushes away a few cobwebs on her way down. When she reaches the last step, she pulls the string on the overhead light.

Her eyes behold a sight that resembles something from Dr. Frankenstein's laboratory, contraptions that would scare the socks off anyone younger than 10. Center stage: a huge barrel topped with a medieval torture device.Overflowing the shelves are strainers, bottles, flasks, tin cups, corks, and an evil-looking iron device with a ratcheted handle. The reason for this odd collection of makeshift equipment and supplies rests on the floor next to the barrel: boxes, boxes, and more boxes of concord grapes—thick-skinned, deep-blue purple grapes with shiny green-globed interiors housing chewy brown seeds.

She is in a winery where the late-summer task of coaxing the juice from the grapes is about to begin.

Calogero leads the vintners down the stairs; they wear white sleeveless tees, bandannas around their sun-tanned necks (they're all in construction—outdoors every day), and concrete-stained work boots—the only casual shoes they own. And who follows behind them? Giuseppina,

Aniella, and Maddelana in their usual multilayered summer finery—front aprons over housedresses.

Concetta stands ready to wash the fruit before it goes through its excruciating cycle in the press. There's a brief tug-of-war between Calogero and Concetta as she singlehandedly lifts a box of grapes. "I can do it myself," she says. She accepts help from no man. In fact, she lowers one end of the crate to free her hand to give Calogero the sign of the *mal'occhio*, the evil eye, to put him in his place.

Aniella, Maddelana, Giuseppina, and Concetta take turns washing the grapes in the deep limestone sink; they deposit the clean fruit in huge galvanized tubs.

"Are we finished here?" Aniella asks.

"Well, maybe," Maddelana says. She has to give a few reminders to the men emptying the tubs of grapes into the barrel. "Last year, you made it too weak. The pastor said it tasted like water."

Giuseppina picks up on the drill. "And the one from Don Ciccio put ours to shame," she says, already ascending the stairs while removing a Chesterfield from its paper pack.

Concetta, drying her hands on her front apron, says, "And don't forget to save two boxes so we can make jelly."

The final muted cry comes from Maddelana at the top of the stairs. "Make sure you make enough to give a few bottles to the nuns."

PEACHES IN RED WINE

Serves four

2 large very ripe peaches, halved
4 teaspoons sugar
1 cup good quality dry red wine

In each of four old-fashioned glasses, place half a peach and 1 teaspoon sugar. Pour an equal amount of red wine over each.

Serve accompanied by a dessert spoon.

PEARS SIMMERED IN RED WINE

Serves four

1½ cups good quality dry red wine
⅓ cup sugar
Pinch of salt
2 cloves
One 1-inch strip lemon peel
2 large pears, peeled, cored, and halved
Hazelnut gelato

Bring first five ingredients to a simmer; cook over medium heat about 5 minutes or until alcohol evaporates.

Add pears; cover; simmer over low heat 10 minutes, or until pears are tender but not soft when pierced with a fork.

Remove pears to serving dishes; over low heat, gently reduce liquid until it thickens and forms a syrup. Remove cloves.

Place a scoop of gelato alongside each pear half; drizzle syrup over pear and gelato; serve.

Preserving the Past

It's a morning at the end of August. Concetta and Maddelana are lucky enough to have a grape arbor lush with filled-to-bursting concord grapes. They pluck the bunches by the stem and deposit the grapes in bushel baskets. Aniella and Giuseppina wait at the fruit stand for workers to unload crates of oozing grapes from a wooden-sided truck. Unlucky grandsons carry the crates home.

After they deposit all the grapes in Concetta's apartment, the four take off for the grocery store to pick up bottles of pectin. Then it's off to the hardware store where they buy preserving jars, sealing wax, funnels, and lengths of cheesecloth. They return to the apartment where bushels and crates of grapes cover every kitchen chair and part of the floor, with a crateful in the sink awaiting a first wash.

Each ties a scarf—a kerchief— around her head, dons an immaculate front apron, scrubs her hands and arms as though preparing to perform surgery, and is ready for an afternoon of washing, simmering, sugaring, and "putting up" the grape jelly to carry her through the winter. They all have the same mission today, so they end up treating one another less like squabbling sisters-in-law, as they usually do, and more like sisters.

The radio is tuned to the Italian station with Donna Lidia offering advice on cheating spouses, complaining mothers-in-law, and of course, ungrateful children. They work in silence so they are sure to catch every solution to every problem. All that they can hear above the sound of Lidia's voice is the cold water running over dozens of bunches of grapes.

When the program ends, they all start to talk at once. "Rinse the cheese-cloth," Concetta orders.

"Get the big white enamel pot," Maddelana adds.

"Measure the sugar," Giuseppina commands.

"I already did," Aniella replies testily.

It's the once-a-year occasion when the nonnas actually measure ingredients—the weights are in pounds—to fill the 12-quart pot. And it's the one day in the year when Giuseppina is forbidden to smoke while they are working.

Simmering grapes, skimming the froth that rises, adding pectin, straining the contents through cheesecloth, filling jars, and melting wax for topping the jars—it all takes hours.

To pass the time, the nonnas reminisce. Concetta reminds the others that she has a monopoly on sadness because she left Italy for Brooklyn when she was 14 years old. "I never saw my mother again."

The others make soothing noises all around. "I know, I know," Aniella says.

A knock on the door interrupts their tales. Concetta's teenage granddaughter and three of the girl's friends, water spotting their dungarees and plaid cotton shirts from their recent visit to the local pool, pile into the house. "Get in the living room right now," Concetta says, shooing them away from the sanitized site of the preserve-making. "Everything here is spotless. We can't have any hair or dirt from outside."

As the girls leave the kitchen, Concetta's granddaughter makes a request. "Okay, when the jelly is ready, you've got to bake the jelly and coconut cake."

Concetta is embarrassed. She bakes the American cake in secret. She is red-faced as the others begin to ask about the cake. "I learned to make it from my daughter," she says.

"Where did she get the recipe?" Giuseppina asks suspiciously. "From a ladies' magazine?"

"I never asked her, but the kids all love it, and so what if it's American?"

"She's right," Aniella says. "We've been here long enough to start making American food. It's not like we're going home again."

"I have a secret when I make it anyway," Concetta says blushing. "I don't use any American white cake. I make it with *pan di espagna*. And nobody knows the difference."

"Of course," they all chorus their approval.

"Make one for our Rosary Society meeting next week," Maddelana says. "You can fool the Irish priest by serving him what he thinks is a *real* American cake."

COCONUT JELLY LAYER CAKE

Serves eight

PAN DI SPAGNA

5 large eggs, room temperature

1 cup sugar

1 teaspoon vanilla extract

Pinch salt

1 cup unbleached, all-purpose flour, sifted 3 times

3 tablespoons butter, softened for coating pans

Preheat oven to 350 degrees F.

Generously butter two 9-inch baking pans; line bottom of pans to within $\frac{1}{4}$-inch of edge with waxed paper or parchment paper; butter paper.

In an electric mixer with whisk attachment, beat eggs with sugar and vanilla until eggs are light-colored, triple in volume, and form a ribbon when beater is lifted.

Fold in flour 2 tablespoons at a time.

Pour batter into pans; bake in lower third of oven 25 to 30 minutes, or until cakes spring back when tapped on top.

Immediately loosen the cake from the side of the pan with a small knife or spatula.

Invert the cake and leave the paper stuck to it.

Turn the cake right-side up and cool it on a wire cooling rack.

FROSTING

2 cups best-quality grape jelly

2 cups sweetened, shredded coconut

ASSEMBLING LAYER CAKE

When cake is cooled completely, remove paper from each layer.

Spread jelly over tops of each layer.

Stack layers; spread jelly over sides.

Sprinkle cake generously on top and sides with coconut.

Covering a Fig Tree

Maddelana, Aniella, and Concetta are in their backyard. Giuseppina arrives dragging a length of rolled-up linoleum—a leftover from the cover on her kitchen floor. They are here to take part in an annual event, the covering of a fig tree to protect it from fall and winter weather. Up and down the block, retirees, grandmas, children, and ladies gather to save the tree and its marvelous fruit for another year.

Calogero and other neighborhood men have already wrapped the tree in wads of newspaper before covering it with the linoleum. Now the women begin to skirt the tree to help tie a length of clothesline and secure the newsprint to the tree.

The trouble starts. Calogero, the group leader and owner of the fig tree, says to Maddelana, "I'll take the rope from you; I can reach the top of the tree." He is telling her gently that her height is a disadvantage.

A nonna never takes "no" from anyone, least of all a man. "Don't tell me how to do this," Maddelana says. "I've been doing this for years!" The leader is resigned. He manages to blurt out, "Yes, but. . . ." before she walks away.

"Good, she's gone," mutters a guy trying to get the job finished. Not so fast.

Maddelana returns with a kitchen chair and places it at the base of the tree. Clutching the trunk, she manages to climb on the chair. She turns around to smile triumphantly at the naysayer as she tugs on the line that someone holds on the other end. Satisfied, she knots her end of the rope.

But the chair starts to totter beneath her. She hesitates. It isn't like her to call for help, certainly not from any of the men there. Fingering her rosary beads in the pocket of her front apron, pressing her shoulder against the half-wrapped tree, she starts gesturing to Giuseppina standing nearby, smoking. She calls to Giuseppina, "Psst, psst, psst. . . ." She can't bring herself to say, "Help me."

Giuseppina looks up and shrugs her shoulders. She can't interpret "Psst, psst" as a cry for help.

Finally Maddelana, floundering on the shaky chair, gestures to Calogero, the man she was putting in his place minutes ago. He smiles and shakes his head. "Here goes," he says. He extends a hand to her and holds onto the chair with his other hand.

Maddelana, red-faced, steps off the chair, points to the line she has looped around the top of the tree, and proclaims, "I did it."

Again, all he has time to say is "Yes, but . . ." before she is off to share news of her victory with the other nonnas. They know she's been unsuccessful in proving her climbing prowess. But Concetta pats her on the shoulder as they all nod in agreement and return to their talk about—what else? Food.

The talk is about the figs the tree bore when it was in bloom. Maddelana wins back the attention of the group as she tells of a recipe bursting with the lush fruit. To ensure her giving them every detail of the recipe, they resort to complimenting her on her chair-bound ballet, her defiance of the group leader, and, of course, her cooking.

"First, you slice a dozen figs in half—longways. . . " Maddelana begins.

......

FIG PIZZA

Serves four

Dough for 1 pizza crust, store-bought or homemade
1 cup whole milk ricotta, well drained
$\frac{1}{2}$ pound whole-milk mozzarella, thinly sliced
$\frac{1}{4}$ pound speck, ham, or prosciutto, thinly sliced, diced
12 figs, halved lengthwise
3 garlic cloves, quartered
3 tablespoons olive oil

6 basil leaves, torn
3 tablespoons Parmigiano Reggiano, grated
1 tablespoon honey
Sprinkle coarse salt
Sprinkle red pepper flakes

Preheat oven to 425 degrees F.

Add olive oil to heated skillet; over medium heat, sauté garlic until golden; set aside oil and garlic.

Spread pizza dough in lightly oiled pizza pan.

Smooth ricotta over dough; top with mozzarella.

Arrange figs in a pinwheel pattern atop mozzarella; sprinkle with speck or ham.

Scatter garlic over ingredients.

Sprinkle pizza with basil, Parmigiano, salt, and pepper.

Drizzle with the remaining garlic oil and honey.

Bake 15 to 20 minutes, or until golden brown and bubbling.

FALL

Problems! Problems!

On a beautiful fall day, Concetta, Maddelana, Aniella, Giuseppina, and the grandchildren arrive at Brooklyn's premier open space, Prospect Park. They let the children run freely in the playground while they sit on a bench—never taking their eyes off the children—and talk about making things right with their world. The neighborhood is rife with grandmas worrying not about the Marshall Plan, or the proliferation of universe-shattering weapons, or the increase in the price of pancetta—even though Concetta has already announced that pancetta has a place in her pasta sauce tonight.

Graver situations give them pause.

Concetta is concerned about Nettie (from the block) finding a fiancé. Maddelana is upset about Mario (the guy who delivers the ice for the icebox) becoming an evangelical. Giuseppina and Aniella are in despair over their neighbor Patrina's recent surgery—even though she's made a full recovery.

They relax as they arrive at solutions to these alarming situations. As long as they can voice an opinion, they believe they have successfully tackled a problem, real or—in Patrina's case—imaginary.

Concetta says, "Nettie should go out with Frankie's brother." They all nod in agreement.

"We should give Mario, the ice-man, a prayer card—get him back to the church," says Maddelana.

Giuseppina deals with the Patrina problem. "Let's visit her just to make sure she *really* looks all right."

"Of course," Aniella says. "Yes, I know these doctors." She pushes her hand out in front as if to ward off the evil bearer of the stethoscope.

After they've packed up all their cares and woes, they sigh, relieved.

And then there is silence. What to talk about now that they have wrestled with and conquered these major issues? "I have to pick up some cream for the pasta tonight," Concetta says. "With some nice peas and pancetta, it's a good dish."

Ah, but in another minute, they are looking upset again. Wherever they turn, the nonnas find something to worry about. This time, it is the care of a neighbor's toddlers as the mother places each child in a swing and gently pushes each one.

"Oh, I can't look," says Concetta. "I'm worried the babies are going to fall out of the swings."

"I'm worried the kids aren't dressed warmly enough," says Maddelana. "Look, they're not wearing hats!"

"Well, there's really nothing we can do about this," Giuseppina says, lighting a Chesterfield. She pauses when the toddlers' mother turns to face her. "Oh, it's Angelina from down the hill. I know her mother."

Knowing Angelina's mother is just the cue the nonnas need to begin their chorus. "Angelina, make sure the babies are strapped in tight," says Concetta.

"What about hats, Angelina?" asks Maddelana. "If I were you, I'd put hats on them so they don't catch cold."

Aniella begins, "And make sure to check them so they're not sitting in a wet diaper. And. . . "

PASTA WITH PEAS AND PANCETTA

Serves four

3 tablespoons dried porcini mushrooms
½ cup pancetta, diced
4 tablespoons olive oil
1 box frozen tiny peas
1 cup heavy cream
Salt and freshly ground pepper to taste
1 pound medium shell pasta, or other ribbed short pasta
¼ cup Parmigiano Reggiano, grated in large shards

Soak mushrooms in 2 cups very hot water for 20 minutes.

Through a strainer and coffee filter or paper towel, drain mushrooms into bowl; dry mushrooms well.

Reserve $\frac{1}{2}$ cup of strained mushroom soaking liquid.

Over medium heat, sauté pancetta in olive oil until crisp and golden; remove pancetta; set aside.

In oil that remains in pan, sauté mushrooms; add peas; stir.

Add $\frac{1}{4}$ cup liquid from soaked mushrooms.

Stir in cream; bring to simmer; do not boil; add salt and pepper; set aside.

Bring 5 quarts water with 2 tablespoons salt to a boil; add pasta.

Cook according to package directions; thoroughly drain pasta.

Return pancetta to pea mixture in sauté pan; stir in pasta; simmer 5 minutes.

If sauce is too thick, add remaining liquid from soaked mushrooms.

Remove pan from heat; sprinkle with cheese; stir and serve.

TV Time

Concetta, Giuseppina, Maddelana, and Aniella can't quite believe that television is coming to their neighborhood. From their vantage point on the stoop, they begin "tsk"-ing whenever they see another antenna attached to a tenement chimney. "I don't like that at all," Concetta says.

"It might fall when I'm on the roof hanging the laundry," Maddelana says. "And it's electric—who knows what it's going to do in a thunderstorm."

"Bah—a television set—it's just another thing to dust and keep clean," Giuseppina says.

"But my daughter Carmella tells me Perry Como has a little show," Aniella says. "Maybe some night we go visit and take a look."

On a Tuesday evening, the four make their way to Carmella's apartment. The living room is crowded with people—on the sofa, on the chairs, on the floor. The crowd spills over into the dining room where chairs face the 10-inch screen television, theater-style, so latecomers can look out over the heads of the crowd seated on the floor.

Grandchildren come forward to kiss and greet Aniella and company. Young fathers vacate chairs directly in front of the set and insist that the nonnas sit. Once seated, they cross their legs at the ankles because their feet do not reach the floor. The crowd, the hubbub, and the offering of drinks from a neighbor they hardly know make the nonnas shy. But people continue to fill the room. There is no getting out.

Carmella enters the room, tells Aniella she's so happy to see them, and begins passing around a tray that holds a bowl of freshly popped corn and several smaller bowls. "Everybody," Carmella announces, "there's red pepper, Parmigiano, brown sugar, and cinnamon to top the corn. Help yourselves."

The nonnas look at one another. Maddelana whispers, "What are we doing here?"

"The food, popcorn!" Giuseppina mutters. "Where's the nice crispy taralli?" Giuseppina and company would prefer Italian crispy "petzels" to snack on. The clink of soft drink bottles passed from person to person drowns out any further complaints.

At eight o'clock, Carmella turns on the set. The crowd is silent at first, but as Milton Berle—Mr. Television—begins his monologue, everyone laughs, except the nonnas. Still, they mind their manners and keep their seats. As the show progresses, Maddelana begins to smile. At one point, Concetta laughs at a doctor joke. By the time Uncle Miltie, wearing lipstick and a riotously flowered dress, faces the camera, the nonnas, especially Giuseppina, are in stitches.

As the show ends, the nonnas assume their poker faces. They make their way out of the living room, stopping only to kiss the grandchildren and the hostess good night.

"Ma, you liked the show?" Carmella asks Aniella.

"It wasn't what we wanted to see," Aniella says, trying to sound disappointed.

"We thought Perry Como was on," Maddelana says.

"He's on Mondays," Carmella says. The nonnas look at one another. What to do? Uncle Miltie was, after all, pretty funny.

Excuses burble out. "I have to visit Aunt Tessie on Monday," Concetta says.

Aniella reacts as if she just remembered something. "Oh, your father works late Monday. I have to stay home to give him dinner."

"Monday," Giuseppina says, "I always babysit for my daughter."

"And I go to the novena at Holy Family," Maddelana says. "I can't miss that."

Aniella turns to Carmella. "I guess that means we'll see you next Tuesday night, okay?"

POPCORN

Serves four

½ cup white or yellow popping corn
3 tablespoons olive oil, not extra virgin
Salt to taste

FOR TOPPING
Grated Parmigiano Reggiano
Mixture brown sugar and cinnamon
Cayenne Pepper
Chili Powder

Pop corn in olive oil according to package directions.

Transfer popcorn to a large bowl; sprinkle with salt.

Pass remaining ingredients to sprinkle on popcorn.

TARALLI

Makes 30

1 package dry yeast
¼ cup warm water
½ cup olive oil
¼ cup dry white wine
2½ cups all-purpose flour, plus 1/4 cup if needed
½ teaspoon salt
3 teaspoons fennel seeds, crushed
3 quarts boiling water

Preheat oven to 350 degrees F.

In a standing mixer with a paddle attachment, dissolve yeast in warm water.

Add remaining ingredients, except boiling water.

Mix to form a soft dough.

Add additional $\frac{1}{4}$ cup flour gradually if needed.

Knead dough 5 to 8 minutes.

Place dough in a clean, lightly oiled bowl and allow to rise until almost double in bulk.

Have ready the deep pot of boiling water.

Divide dough into walnut-size balls.

Form each ball into a thin strip about 7 inches long by rolling on a board or in the palms of your hands; each strip should be a bit thicker than a strand of spaghetti.

Form the strips of dough into circles (about 2 inches around), knotting the ends.

Drop the rings a few at a time into the boiling water for 1 to 2 minutes, or until each ring floats to the top; remove with slotted spoon.

Allow to dry for a few minutes on a parchment-lined baking sheet.

Lightly coat a baking sheet with olive oil.

Place rounds on sheet; bake 20 minutes, or until golden.

The Macaroni's in the Basement—The Wake is Upstairs

There's been a death on Concetta's block, the husband of a neighbor. In the neighborhood, someone might die after a prolonged illness or with the good fortune to "drop dead after work on his way home from the subway." In either case, a wake consumes the following week.

So much to do, so much to do. The outfits come first. "Go buy a new pair of black stockings for me," Concetta commands, addressing whichever teenage girl—niece, granddaughter, or neighbor—is in the house.

Maddalena's neighbor across the street has worn black for the last 25 years. First, her husband died. Then her cousin "passed away." Four years ago, her mother's aunt died. Then her sister-in-law's brother (whom she's never met) died in Naples (or as it's familiarly referred to "on the other side"). As a perpetual mourner, she has so many black dresses, coats, suits, and hats she might look right at home taking a job on Fifth Avenue.

Younger women in the family dig into closets, run downtown to shop, or borrow from neighbors to get back in black. Amid all this activity, they discuss one thing. How long do we have to wear this? There is a sliding scale: a husband, many, many years; a parent, one year; a cousin, several months; and a brother-in-law, three to four weeks at most.

After family and friends are done up in Zorro-like attire, their main concern is the food. Any funeral home in a post-War Italian American neighborhood houses a kitchen in the basement.

Wherever a wake is taking place, recruiting cooks to prepare meals is a piece of cake. Concetta begs for the privilege; Aniella pleads; Maddelana insists; even Giuseppina makes a half-hearted offer. The meals they plan to prepare for the family and visitors will bring instant acclaim to the would-be chefs. Their train of gravy will carry them on to glory. So in fairness, the family of the deceased select Concetta, Aniella, Maddelana, and yes, Giuseppina to alternate and prepare dinners during the four-day event.

Maddelana quietly reminds Giuseppina, "Remember, no smoking in the kitchen at the wake, okay?"

"Bah, you know cooking is not my favorite thing," Giuseppina says.

Those who are not at the stove sit upstairs; they weep and shout out the name of the loved one every five minutes, throwing in an occasional *buon'anima* (good soul, or may he rest in peace). Nevermore will the deceased be known simply as "Jimmy;" even 30 years after his wake, he will still be known as "*buon'anima* Jimmy."

The call to dinner brings family, friends, and children, ages 18 months to 18 years, to the table in the basement. The main course: macaroni with gravy, always, every night. While dishes are passed around, the cook *del giorno*, arms folded across her chest, stands beaming and waiting for the word that her macaroni is better than the one served the night before.

After the funeral Mass, as they leave the church, Concetta, Maddelana, Aniella, and Giuseppina regard one another with both suspicion and satisfaction. Each has heard from the family, unbeknown to the others, that her dish was the best.

MACARONI AND GRAVY

Serves eight

FOR THE MEAT
1 cup plus $\frac{1}{4}$ cup red wine
2 pounds Italian sausage, a mix of hot and sweet with fennel
2 tablespoons olive oil
2 cloves garlic, peeled and quartered
3 pounds baby-back ribs, sliced into serving pieces
Salt and freshly ground pepper to taste

Heat large skillet over high heat; reduce heat; add wine; bring to a simmer.

Pierce sausage all over with the point of a knife; add to simmering wine.

Simmer sausage, turning frequently until all wine evaporates and sausage browns in its own fat; remove sausage and set aside.

Reduce heat to medium; add olive oil.

Dry ribs; sprinkle with salt and freshly ground pepper.

Add ribs and garlic to skillet; sauté garlic until golden; set aside.

Brown ribs on all sides about 20 minutes; set aside.

Deglaze pan with the $\frac{1}{4}$ cup wine.

FOR THE GRAVY
4 tablespoons olive oil
2 cloves garlic, peeled and quartered
2 tablespoons tomato paste
3 tablespoons raisins
1 cup dry red wine
$\frac{1}{4}$ cup fresh basil, thinly sliced, or 3 teaspoons dried
2 tablespoons fresh rosemary leaves, chopped, or 2 teaspoons dried
2 bay leaves
Sprinkle of crushed red pepper flakes
1 teaspoon fennel seeds
Salt and freshly ground pepper to taste
2 cans San Marzano tomatoes
1 can water
2 cans tomato sauce

While ribs are browning, heat a large casserole over high heat; add olive oil.

Reduce heat to low; add garlic and tomato paste, salt and pepper.

Simmer slowly, stirring often for 10 minutes.

Add 1 cup wine, raisins, and herbs, to tomato paste mixture.

Simmer until wine is reduced by half.

Add tomatoes, water, and tomato sauce; bring to a boil; reduce heat to low; simmer, uncovered 20 minutes.

Bring sauce back to boil; add reduced wine from skillet, ribs and sausage; reduce heat to simmer.

Partially cover sauce; simmer over very low heat 3 to 4 hours.

FOR SERVING
1 pound fusilli, perciatelli, or other long thick pasta.
Parmigiano reggiano, freshly grated

Bring 5 quarts of highly salted water to a boil; stir in macaroni; cook macaroni until al dente; drain well.

Remove meat and half the gravy from the casserole to a serving dish

Stir macaroni into sauce in casserole; simmer for about five minutes over low heat. Serve macaroni with the additional sauce and meat on the side.

Pass the Parmigiano at the table.

The World at Their Doorstep

Concetta and Aniella leave their apartments to shop for food and fabric, to pay their respects at wakes, to have coffee with one another, and of course to make novenas and go to Mass. Giuseppina ventures out to visit her friends and to buy cigarettes. Like Maddelana, who leaves every day to clean a church in far-flung neighborhoods, the four also throw in a spare afternoon to clean their church. Aside from these obligations, they rarely have to walk out the front door, because much of the business comes to them.

Today in Concetta's kitchen, it is business as usual as three are sipping coffee and Giuseppina is sipping tea from a glass resting next to an ashtray that is rapidly filling up. She is about to list her latest ailments when there is a knock at the door.

Representing the world of finance, a stocky insurance agent, huffing and puffing, has made his way to Concetta's third-floor apartment, interrupting the nonnas' talk about what to cook for dinner. He is there to collect a weekly premium—usually 25 cents, sometimes less, but never more than 30 cents—for a term-life insurance policy.

The women welcome him as he places his gray fedora on a chair, unbuttons his heavy overcoat, and takes a seat at the table.

He accepts a cup of coffee —American—with milk and sugar. The nonnas smile, hands folded across their laps, as they wait for the "news" the agent is about to deliver. He is the town crier, presenting neighborhood gossip along with a receipt, after he records the payment in a ledger held together with a thick rubber band.

"So what's new?" Concetta asks, offhandedly. He verifies the rumor that the man who drives in from New Jersey every Wednesday to deliver eggs door-to-door has, in fact, run off with a local Irish widow.

"Oh, thank heavens she had no children," Aniella says, half blessing herself.

"But what about the eggs?" Giuseppina asks. She is relieved to learn that the elopee's brother-in-law, his sister's husband, is going to continue to deliver the eggs.

At the table, Maddelana pulls from her apron pocket a three-by-five-inch carbon receipt for a purchase she made in her living room. "Today when the salesman from the religious store visited, I bought a statue of the Infant of Prague in a satin gown." She is blissful as she holds court at the table. "With the scraps I have left over from sewing, I'll make him a lace gown," she says.

The clanging bell of the scissor sharpener's truck distracts them as they bid the agent good-bye. Concetta accepts a carbon copy of the insurance receipt, then goes to the window, opens it wide, and shouts, "Over here, third floor." The sharpener stops his truck and enters the building.

When he reaches the apartment, Concetta hands him three pairs of scissors. She warns him to take special care. "One is a hair-cutter," she says. "One is thin and fine for embroidery, and my favorite is the one I use for cutting fabric."

He leaves with the shears in hand, telling her they are sure to be "like brand-new in 20 minutes." On the stairs, he passes the one man who canvasses every apartment in the building. He needs no appointment; he is the Fuller Brush man. The Queens of Clean can never purchase too many mops, brooms, bottle brushes, vegetable brushes, hair brushes, and—to complete the circle—new mop heads. As the nonnas welcome him, they all begin talking at once.

"That hairbrush, the one I bought last week?" Giuseppina says. He knows this woman is fierce when she is disappointed. He looks a little worried, fearing the bad news she might deliver. "That brush is so nice," she says. "It doesn't pull my granddaughter's hair, no matter how I brush it."

The nonnas' kitchens become their offices, repair shops, boutiques, and janitors' closets. Roasting peppers for supper, they welcome the pie man who supplies them with dessert. Sitting and sipping coffee, they pass judgment on the day's business.

"He did a good job on the scissors," Concetta says.

"I'm glad the egg man's brother-in-law will still deliver the eggs," Maddelana says.

"The insurance man is a nice fellow for telling us about the egg man," Giuseppina says, stubbing out a cigarette.

"He always has the latest news," Aniella agrees.

Not much business takes place in a tenement on a Saturday morning. But still the nonnas have a way to spend money at home—for entertainment. Instead of paying insurance men, purveyors of statues, and salesmen of brushes, they toss coins to an organ grinder who sets up camp in front of the building. As they lean out open windows, their elbows cushioned by pillows, they listen and smile.

ONIONS AND EGGS

Serves four

3 tablespoons olive oil
1 pound onions, thinly sliced
Dash salt
Dash sugar
8 large eggs
Salt and freshly ground pepper to taste

Heat a large nonstick skillet; add olive oil.

Add onions, salt, and sugar; reduce heat to medium.

Sauté onions 25 minutes, or until golden brown and reduced by half.

Beat eggs just until whites and yolks are combined.

Reduce heat to low.

Pour eggs into skillet; allow eggs to set for 1 minute.

Sprinkle with salt and pepper.

Stir and fold eggs into onions for about 6 minutes, or until eggs form large, tender curds.

Serve immediately on a plate or as a sandwich filling.

The Statue's Eyes Moved—Really

It is a usual fall Friday afternoon in the parish church. The eighth-grade girls, ready to help the nuns and the sacristan with the weekly cleaning, have entered from the side door. The early arrivals, Concetta, Giuseppina, Maddelana, and Aniella, are already hard at work—kerchiefs tied around their heads, sweat on their upper lips, and feather dusters in hand.

Maddelana has even set up an ironing board in the sacristy, the better to iron the lace-trimmed linen altar cloths. They work swiftly so they can get to the fish market, then back to their kitchens to prepare the Friday night fish dinner.

As the girls arrive, Giuseppina follows Concetta, dusting the wonderfully detailed Stations of the Cross that grace either side of the church. In place of hats, the girls wear tissues bobby-pinned to their hair; they cross in front of the altar several times as they scrub the frieze that supports the altar itself and genuflect each time they pass the tabernacle. The nuns are in the sacristy arranging bunches of pom-poms and Fuji chrysanthemums for the altar.

Surrounded by the scent of lemon polish, beeswax candles, and starched linen, Maddelana smiles as she goes about her tasks. It is tough work for her at a majestic height of 5 feet 2 inches to reach the noses of the statues she dusts, never mind whisking the halos. Still, she swipes as best she can the beards and sometimes even the ears of the martyrs. And as she dusts, she stops to light a candle and say a prayer in front of each of her favorite saints.

Suddenly a scream rings out. An eighth grader prying wax from used candleholders follows her scream with a shout. "I saw it; I saw it!" she proclaims loudly but reverently. "I saw Saint Anne's eyes following me."

Nuns and nonnas come running. They calm the girl with hugs and reassurance that the "movement" is only a trick of the light. She accepts their ministrations and goes on to the next bank of candles. The nuns enter the sacristy, and the nonnas continue their tasks.

The girls leave early on these short fall days to get home before dark. The nuns return to the convent. Only the nonnas remain standing in front of the statue of Saint Anne as twilight filters through the stained-glass windows.

Giuseppina looks around to make sure they are the only ones left. Then she nudges Concetta. "Here, see for yourself," she says quietly. "They really are moving."

Concetta pauses. "I saw it myself first, but I didn't want to upset everyone." With that, she gets to her knees, pulls rosary beads from her apron pocket, and begins to pray.

"What do you mean, you saw it yourself?" demands Maddelana. "I was here before you; not only did they move, they blinked." She falls to her knees and begins saying a rosary of her own.

"You know Saint Anne spoke to me when I first got here," Aniella boasts. "She said, 'Tell them I'm going to move my eyes today.'" And then Aniella kneels, rosary beads in hand. "These kids," she says, shaking her head. "They think they know everything. But we show them, eh?"

VENETIAN FRIDAY FISH

Serves four

1¼ pounds lemon sole, flounder, petrale, or grey sole
Salt and freshly ground pepper to taste
½ cup unbleached flour
¼ cup olive oil
2 tablespoons red wine vinegar
¼ teaspoon red pepper flakes
1 small red onion, thinly sliced into rings

Rinse and dry fish; sprinkle with salt and pepper; dust fish with flour; shake off excess.

Heat a broad skillet; add oil; when oil is hot, sauté fish until golden on each side.

Transfer fish to a flat plate; sprinkle with vinegar and red pepper; scatter onion rings atop fish. Serve at room temperature.

Photographic Memories

On a rainy fall afternoon, Giuseppina, Maddelana, and Aniella are having coffee in Concetta's kitchen. In the next room, separated only by a doorway, their grandchildren are turning the pages of old photo albums and rifling through loose black-and-whites. A grandson rushes in and waves a photo at Concetta.

"Who's this, Nonna?" the child asks.

"He's great grandma's brother," she says. "He never came to America. He . . . "

Satisfied, the boy returns to his place among the albums. But in seconds, a granddaughter stumbles under the weight of an album as she enters the kitchen. "Who are all these soldiers?" she asks.

"Oh, let me see," Maddelana says.

"No, me first," Giuseppina says. Each reaches out to claim the album that holds photos of their sons, their sons' friends, and the neighborhood's only West Point graduate—a commissioned officer. They begin to pass the album around. When Aniella lingers on a page, Giuseppina elbows her and tells her to "move on."

"Never mind," the girl says and starts to leave empty handed to join her brother in the next room.

"Wait," Concetta calls to her. "This is your father when he was in the Army."

"Come and see," she calls to her brother. "Here, look at all Daddy's medals." They take a look and quickly run back to the photos they are separating from the pile and stealthily removing from albums—recent photos of themselves.

At the table, the nonnas laugh at images of now bald sons-in-law, images captured when the men had full heads of dark curls. "Look, there's the block party when they all came back home," Maddelana says.

"That's the one we made the special lasagna Genovese for," Concetta says. On they go, laughing and pointing.

Then silence falls. Each simply crosses herself as she looks at a photo of a young man smiling proudly in his uniform. "He was nineteen, Nino—in the Pacific," Maddelana says. "God rest his soul." She gently closes the book. They dab at their eyes.

The squabbling of the children in the next room breaks the silence. "Hey, don't fight with your sister," Concetta scolds. "Come and have some milk and cake."

The girl enters the kitchen carrying an album covered in white satin. She manages to hold her fingers between two thick pages to mark her place.

"Here I am," she says, handing the album to Giuseppina. "I'm the flower girl, see?" She passes around the album showing a photo of a post-World War II wedding.

"Oh, you were so beautiful," Concetta says happily, her eyes tearing. "They all waited to get married until after the War. But some, like Nino, didn't see the War end." She sighs.

Each nonna pinches the children's cheeks, gently ruffles their hair, and hugs them. Silently, they understand: no collateral damage here. They nod in agreement.

LASAGNA GENOVESE

Serves ten

PESTO

3 cups basil leaves
2 cloves garlic, minced
$\frac{1}{2}$ cup Parmigiano Reggiano cheese, roughly grated
$1\frac{1}{4}$ to $1\frac{1}{2}$ cups extra virgin olive oil
3 tablespoons toasted pine nuts
$\frac{1}{2}$ teaspoon salt
$\frac{1}{2}$ teaspoon freshly ground pepper
Dried red pepper flakes to taste

In blender or food processor, pulse all ingredients, until sauce is thick and creamy.

Add more oil if necessary; set aside.

LASAGNA

1 pound curly edge lasagna noodles

10 fingerling potatoes, scrubbed, thinly sliced, steamed in salted water
until tender

1 pound green beans, sliced on the bias, steamed in salted water 5 minutes

1 cup Parmigiano Reggiano, coarsely grated

1 pound whole milk mozzarella, diced

2 pounds whole-milk ricotta, drained

2 large eggs, beaten

3 tablespoons flat-leaf parsley, minced

Salt and freshly ground pepper to taste

Pesto

Preheat oven to 375 degrees F.

Boil noodles in salted water, according to package directions;
drain well.

Blend mozzarella, ricotta, and eggs with parsley; add salt and
pepper to taste.

Layer pesto, noodles, green beans, grated cheese, potatoes, blended
cheeses, and pesto.

Continue stacking ingredients in the same order, ending with
noodles, pesto, and a sprinkling of Parmigiano.

Cover loosely with aluminum foil; bake 35 minutes; remove foil;
bake 10 minutes, or until golden brown.

Let rest 15 to 20 minutes before serving.

Piecework

Concetta, Aniella, Maddelana, and Giuseppina arrive at the storefront factory at 8:45am. Each carries a paper lunch bag filled with last night's leftovers, no matter what they are (even pasta turns up), stuffed into a sandwich. They greet one another as the forelady (whom they call the floorlady) distributes the sleeves, yokes, and facings that will become parts of a full-length quilted robe.

At 9am, the mothers (daughters of the nonnas) rush in, fresh from seeing their children off to school. Each mother rushes to kiss her mother. Finally, the machines and the chatter begin to whir. "A nickel a sleeve," Aniella grumbles. "We deserve twice as much."

"Ma, get to work," her daughter Carmella replies. "I don't have time for this right now."

"What do you mean, you don't have time to listen to your mother?" Giuseppina asks. And *her* daughter tells her, "Knock it off. It's not your business."

In the meantime, the teams—mothers and daughters—deftly encourage straight seams to glide across each machine. All work in silence for a while. That is, until the boss turns the radio dial to her favorite Italian soap opera. "Ah," say Concetta and Madeline, who get a kick out of the continuing tales of love lost, found, dead, reborn, or supernatural.

"Bah," many of the daughters mutter. The radio actors drone in counterpoint to the noise of the machines.

When the show ends and the machines fall silent, the workers snip threads, turn sleeves rightside out, and pass work on to the pressers. This way, the mothers *and* daughters can listen attentively to the next radio program. This is Donna Lidia, the queen of advice—given in Italian—about real-life problems of love lost, found, dead, reborn, or supernatural.

Donna Lidia reads the letters asking for help. "My husband spends too much time with his friends and not enough time with me," one listener writes. Another writes, "I think my daughter-in-law is running around." And the most compelling letter states, "My daughter is in love with my third cousin's nephew on his father's side, but my third cousin and I are not speaking."

Lidia puts her heart and soul into her voice as she coaxes, wheedles, and cajoles the audience into accepting her solutions and opinions. And the nonnas and mothers nod their heads in agreement.

At noon, Giuseppina, Maddelana, Aniella, and Concetta stand, sigh, and reach into their lunch bags. Each takes a piece of carefully wrapped fruit out of her bag and deposits the fruit on the machine of a nonna who has returned after a leave for a death in her family.

The daughters rush out to pick up their children from school and take them home for lunch. They engage in a marathon sprint to meet the children, feed them, get them back to school, and get themselves back to work.

The afternoon passes as the talk turns to food. "It's Monday; I have leftover chicken soup," Aniella says.

"I'll make some spiedini for the kids," Concetta says.

"Cold chicken from yesterday," Giuseppina says. Then each extends an invitation to her daughter to dine at her house after work.

The nonnas make it clear that their daughters are not to take dinner invitations lightly.

"Your sister is dying to see you," Aniella says.

"Your father's waiting all week for you to visit," says Maddelana.

But there is one weapon in their arsenal of guilt that is sure to make a daughter say, "Yes, I'll be there."

"I never get to see your kids anymore," says Concetta, "And I'm fixing the spiedini just for them." The daughter knows she's been bested. Satisfied, Concetta goes back to her stitching.

SPIEDINI

Serves four

2 pounds thinly sliced sirloin or rib steak, pounded very thin
¼ cup plus 2 tablespoons olive oil
1 onion, finely minced
1 cup fresh bread crumbs
12 bay leaves
Salt and freshly ground pepper to taste

Preheat oven to 400 degrees F.

In a skillet, heat ¼ cup oil; add onions; sauté until limp.

Add bread crumbs; sauté until onions and crumbs are golden.

Add salt and pepper to taste

Slice steak into 12 strips about 2 inches wide and 4 inches long

Spoon a tablespoon of filling on each strip; roll each strip into a pinwheel.

Use a toothpick or skewer to fasten a bay leaf to each roll.

Brush the rolls and a rimmed sheet pan with the remaining oil.

Lightly sprinkle rolls with salt and pepper.

Bake 12 to 14 minutes or until nicely browned.

Remove skewer and bay leaf from each before serving.

Homework

Aniella, Maddelana, Giuseppina, and Concetta like to have their own money set aside in covered sugar bowls. They use the money for treats for grandchildren, for special gifts for their husbands' birthdays, and of course, for the yards of yarn and fabric they need to crochet, knit, and sew. Pinafores for granddaughters are all the rage, and their machines whirr as they make one for each little girl in the family.

Besides their regular jobs, they earn some money doing homework that the neighborhood factories farm out—stringing beads for necklaces and bracelets, crocheting pocketbooks in a multicolor pineapple stitch, or sewing trimming on almost-finished garments. At the end of each week, jobbers pick up the work and deliver a new batch, together with a small manila envelope filled with cash for last week's work.

Each nonna works exclusively in her own kitchen. This Friday afternoon, Aniella is creating elaborate iridescent necklaces. Her helpers: her daughter Carmella and a preteen granddaughter. Each knots the end of a length of waxed thread after drawing it through a needle. They add a metal tip to keep the beads from rolling off the thread. Then they begin: add one bead; tie a knot; add a second bead; tie a knot—until the thread is covered with iridescent "pearls."

Aniella adds a filigree clasp to each strand and fastens the necklaces closed. She places each finished glowing beauty into its own satin-lined, midnight-blue velvet box and sets it next to other velvet boxes in a carton that the jobber picks up when he delivers work.

Dusting her hands together signals that the day's work is complete. Aniella fixes a snack—coffee for her and Carmella, warm milk with a tablespoon of coffee and two sugars, and an egg biscuit for her granddaughter.

"It's hard to make something without meat every Friday," Aniella complains. "How many fish can I cook?"

"Oh, Ma, please," her daughter says. "You can make pasta with almost anything—peas, fish, beans, cheese, broccoli, or just garlic and oil—and you have a meal."

"Well, I still find this no meat, not too nice."

There is a knock on the door and Concetta enters. She kisses Carmella, pinches the granddaughter's cheeks, and says to the girl, "You're getting so tall—like a beanpole." The girl looks away and rolls her eyes.

"I hate to ask, but do you have any eggs in the house?"

"Sure, sure," Aniella answers. "How many?"

"I need six, but I only have four." She helps herself to coffee and sits at the table, beginning her own what-to-cook on Friday litany. "I don't mind not cooking meat, but I run out of ideas, and Father Anthony is coming over for dinner."

"So, you're going to make a frittata with potatoes?"

"No. I'm going to make the perfect Friday dish. It shows how I feel about not roasting a chicken—eggs in purgatory."

The granddaughter looks shocked. Carmella stifles a laugh, and Aniella says, "Good for you."

EGGS IN PURGATORY

Serves four

4 tablespoons olive oil

2 cloves garlic, peeled, thinly sliced

Two cups tomato sauce, store-bought or homemade

Salt and freshly ground pepper to taste

6 large eggs

2 tablespoons fresh basil, torn, or 1 teaspoon dried

$\frac{1}{4}$ cup Parmigiano Reggiano, grated (optional)

6 slices country bread, toasted

In a large nonstick skillet, heat olive oil.

Add garlic; sauté until golden; stir in tomatoes, salt, and pepper.

Simmer 15 minutes, or until sauce thickens slightly.

Using a tablespoon, make six depressions in the sauce.

Break eggs, one at a time, onto a small, flat dish; gently slide each egg into a depression in the sauce; do not break yolks.

Cover pan; simmer 7 to 9 minutes, or until whites are set and yolks remain soft.

Sprinkle with basil; place each egg with some sauce atop a slice of toast.

Serve cheese for sprinkling if desired.

Sewing for Fun

Concetta, Maddelana, Aniella, and Giuseppina sew piecework in a factory five days a week to earn a living; they sew for their family at home in the evenings and on weekends to relax. Once they lay out the pattern and pin it to the fabric, they are convinced that the work is practically finished. It does not matter that they have not sewn a stitch. The most challenging parts of the operation—purchasing the pattern and selecting the fabric, or "material" as they call it—are tasks they liken to pushing a large boulder up a mountain. When they are satisfied with their purchases, they have won the battle.

On this cold fall evening, the battle is beginning. The nonnas are in the dry goods store to pick out patterns, compare cottons and corduroys, match thread to fabric, and search for contrasting rickrack. Each is leafing through a pattern book selecting a pattern for a dress for a granddaughter. They are being extra-courteous to one another since Maddelana and Concetta have already had a tiny tiff over who would get the pattern for the dress with the Peter Pan collar. The dispute resolved itself when there was only one pattern left in the size they each needed and Concetta grabbed it first. But emotions are still simmering as they make their way down the narrow aisles filled with bolts of fabric.

Concetta must be wary. The bolt she is pulling by its end from the table may have been seized at its other end by, say, Giuseppina. Whoever eyed it first should have first dibs, but nonnas believe that they simply must have whatever appeals to another. A tug of war ensues until Giuseppina spies another bolt, leaving Concetta holding onto the bolt that wavers like a strand of overcooked spaghetti.

The owner of the store remains unruffled as he follows the nonnas around, rolling up the lengths of fabric they have unrolled to measure the yardage. Their measuring stick? The distance between the nose and the fingertips at the end of an extended arm. The technique gives them an almost harem dancer look as they cover their mouths with the fabric.

For the nonnas, buying fabric by the yard is only okay. What they really seek are remnants, end-of-bolt pieces that they can claim for a dollar or less. The owner is aware of their scheme as he hurriedly makes his way to place those remnants with the most yardage at the bottom of the pile, leaving Concetta and Giuseppina to dangle skimpy quarter-yard pieces in their hands. All the while, they curse their stars that they are unable to find any two-yard or three-yard pieces. Gloom turns to triumph when one of them notices a thick edge of folded fabric sticking out of the bottom of a pile. Discovering gold in their own backyards would not be as gratifying as ferreting out a remnant of printed percale.

Each carries a bolt or a remnant as she makes her way to the cutting table. Now the craftiness of these crafters comes into play. "The edge is crooked there," Giuseppina says to the young girl measuring. "So you have to allow for that. Maybe add on another, say, eighth of a yard—free, please."

The owner, seeing the sales assistant's baffled look, says to her, "I'll take care of these lovely ladies myself." Although he isn't Italian, he repeatedly "*signoras*" the nonnas until they melt. He has bested them without giving away even an extra half-inch of fabric.

When they leave the store and are walking up the hill, they quibble a bit over whose house they are going to for coffee. Giuseppina does not enter into the discussion. She is too busy trying to light a Chesterfield in the brisk autumn breeze.

"I made Regina cookies," Concetta says.

The rest start talking all together, all at once. "Yes, okay," Aniella says.

"That's fine," Maddelana says. "Not too much trouble if we come over?"

"No, we can look at the pattern—you know, the one with the Peter Pan collar—while I'm making coffee," she says, needling Giuseppina.

REGINA COOKIES

Makes 24

$1\frac{1}{2}$ cups flour
$\frac{1}{2}$ cup corn meal
2 teaspoons baking powder
$\frac{1}{4}$ teaspoon salt
1 stick unsalted butter at room temperature
$\frac{1}{2}$ cup sugar
2 large eggs, beaten well, plus 1 egg yolk
1 tablespoon milk
1 teaspoon pure vanilla extract
$\frac{1}{4}$ teaspoon pure almond extract
1 cup sesame seeds

Preheat oven to 350 degrees F.

In the oven, lightly toast sesame seeds 6 minutes; remove to flat plate; allow to cool.

Mix dry ingredients together; set aside.

Combine the egg yolk with the milk; beat well; set aside.

Cream butter, sugar, and extracts together; add remaining eggs; combine well.

Add flour mixture; beat well.

Divide dough into 4 pieces; roll each piece into a log; cut each log into six 3-inch pieces.

Brush each piece with combined egg-and-milk mixture; roll each in sesame seeds.

Place cookies on parchment-lined baking sheet.

Bake 20 minutes, or until golden brown.

Place cookies on wire rack to cool.

Church Ladies

Concetta, Aniella, and Maddelana clutch their black cloth coats tightly to keep out the fall wind as they assemble on a Wednesday night on a corner near the church. While they wait for the perpetually tardy Giuseppina, they talk about what they made for dinner. "So cold today, I made ribollita," Concetta says. "I'll serve the leftovers tomorrow."

"We had sausage and peppers," Aniella says. "My daughter stayed to eat with us."

"Ah, here she is," Maddelana says. They all turn to see Giuseppina smoking but rushing, as best she can, to catch up with them. "Next time, don't keep us waiting, okay?" Maddelana says to her sister.

Following that warning, the nonnas set out for the church. They enter, dip their fingers in the font, make a sign of the cross, kiss it up to heaven, find their pew, genuflect, and sit down with a sigh. Going to church isn't easy.

They are here to make a novena. A novena is a ritual of prayer and song observed nine times—nine hours, nine days, or nine weeks. It's an ongoing weekly service in every parish, giving congregants a chance to complete any nine services according to their own schedule.

Novenas are offered to many saints. The nonnas, super-novena-goers, attend the one devoted to Saint Anthony. Showing up every Wednesday over thirty years, they have completed more than a thousand novenas each. It is customary to make a request and pray to the saint to grant a wish. Concetta has prayed for wars to end. Maddelana has prayed for her neighbors' children to get out of jail. Aniella has prayed for her sons to find work. Giuseppina has prayed for her daughters to have healthy babies. They all pray for their grandsons' girlfriends to stop acting tarty. And since all these things come to pass eventually, the nonnas are convinced that their novenas are "working."

The service remains the same from week to week. The prayers they recite by heart, the hymns they sing softly. But this night is different. The priest who enters the sanctuary is not Father Al, Father Jim, or even Monsigner the Pastor. (He *does* preside at a novena occasionally.) Tonight's priest is a sandaled, brown-garbed monk.

The nonnas elbow one another and furrow their brows. Giuseppina quietly asks in Italian, "Who is this guy?'

The others shrug. They are baffled. But worse than that, they are being subject to CHANGE, something they have hoped—and in this case prayed—would never happen in their lives.

The monk steps into the pulpit and asks all to rise. The nonnas do. He begins to pray in heavily accented English. The nonnas listen, and before they add their "Amen," they become almost giddy.

"He's from Italy," Maddelana whispers.

"Oh, yes." Concetta says, "Look, he looks like Saint Francis—or maybe Saint Anthony."

Instead of a homily, the monk offers an explanation for his presence. He is collecting funds to help orphaned children in his town, near Naples, in the province of Campania.

The clasps on their pocketbooks snap loudly as Concetta, Guiuseppina, and Maddelana dig in to find their change purses. Giuseppina debates with Concetta in whispers. "You know Aniella is Sicilian."

Concetta says, "Will she give money for something in Campania?" An usher approaches with the collection basket. The change the three nonnas dump in the basket makes a lot of noise when it reaches bottom. The usher is about to move on when Aniella dips her hand into her coat pocket. She waves the one-dollar bill she takes from her pocket high enough for all to see. She deposits it in the basket, and it doesn't make a sound. Satisfied, she dusts her hands together.

The others nod, pleased. Maddelana reaches for Aniella's hand. She waves Maddelana's hand away and says, "Bah."

RIBOLLITA

Serves eight to ten (excellent reheated)

3 large Idaho or other baking potatoes, peeled, sliced in chunks
3 carrots, peeled, diced
1 large onion, diced
6 tablespoons olive oil
Salt
Freshly ground pepper
3½ quarts boiling water
1½ cups elbow macaroni or other small pasta
1 box frozen corn
1 box frozen peas
1 can chickpeas, drained and well rinsed
1 can pink kidney beans, drained and well rinsed
1 can cannellini beans, drained and well rinsed
2 slices country bread, in small dice

SEASONING INGREDIENTS
1 large bunch basil, finely minced, or 1 tablespoon dried basil
2 tablespoons tomato paste
6 tablespoons olive oil
Crushed red pepper flakes
2 cloves garlic, finely minced
Salt
Freshly ground pepper
Shards of Reggiano Parmigiano or Asiago cheese (optional)
Additional crushed red pepper flakes (optional)

SOUP

Heat olive oil in a heavy nonreactive stockpot.

Add potatoes, carrots, and onion; sprinkle liberally with salt and pepper; add bay leaf.

Sauté vegetables over medium heat, stirring often, about 20 minutes, or until golden.

Pour boiling water over vegetables; bring to a boil over high heat; stir.

Reduce heat to medium-low; partially cover pot; simmer soup 45 minutes.

Over high heat, return soup to the boil; add pasta; stir.

Reduce heat to medium; simmer 10 minutes or until pasta is almost cooked.

Add corn, peas, and all beans.

Simmer 8 minutes over medium heat, or until corn and peas are cooked.

Break bread into very fine pieces; crumble into soup; stir.

Incorporate bread bits into soup by pressing them against the side of the pot.

Remove pot from heat; fold in seasoning.

SEASONING

In a small bowl, combine tomato paste, olive oil, basil, salt, pepper, red pepper flakes, and garlic.

Fold seasoning mixture into soup.

Serve soup with grated cheese and red pepper flakes if desired.

A Storefront Caravan

"In a quaint caravan, there's a lady they call the Gypsy," the song says. In South Brooklyn at autumn's end, the quaint caravan isn't a brightly colored circus trailer set up for temporary living. It's a storefront. Any vacant storefront on an avenue can become home to the lady and her family—the Gypsies.

Heavy red and gold drapes hang in the window of their new home, a former tailor shop. The drapes fail to meet in the center, leaving just enough room for people to peek in while passing by. The opulent curtains seem at odds with a very visible canvas-covered ironing board affixed to one wall.

The gap in the window covering serves as a magnet attracting grandsons in the neighborhood. On their way to school, on their way to buy a quart of milk, on their way to climb the schoolyard fence, they stop and stare.

Outside the doorway of a nearby vegetable store, Concetta and Maddelana meet. Concetta sees three boys looking in the window of what they still call "the tailor's." She shouts at the boys, "Get away from there!"

The boys make a show of covering their eyes and scoot around the corner.

And this gives Concetta and Maddelana the chance they have been waiting for, *their* opportunity to discuss the Gypsies. The topic of the neighborhood newcomers has almost replaced the nonnas' favorite subject—food.

"We don't know what goes on in there," Maddelana says. She motions toward the storefront home.

"I notice the young man this morning," Concetta says and lowers her voice. "He wears an earring." She raises her eyebrows and shakes her head in disapproval. But it's only mild disapproval. "You should see the good job he did fixing that fender on my son's truck."

"But the old woman worries me," Maddelana says. "She tells fortunes. Of course, my daughter-in-law is always first in line to hear what the Gypsy has to say."

"Did her fortune come true?"

"Well, the old woman told my daughter-in-law that she was going to have a baby," Maddelana says. "That wasn't a surprise. She was already seven months pregnant."

Their conversation is interrupted when they see a toddler running out of the tailor shop. The girl starts moving toward the street, and Concetta and Maddelana make a dash for her. Concetta reaches for the girl when she is inches from the curb.

The old woman and the girl's mother rush out of the store to pick up the girl and to thank the nonnas.

Concetta nods knowingly but says nothing as she passes the girl to her mother. She waves her hand in dismissal when the mother thanks her.

Maddelana is uncharacteristically quiet as she breathes in a spicy scent. She turns to the younger woman. "What are you cooking?" she asks.

"Paprikash," the woman answers. "It's a stew with meat and vegetables and paprika." She recites the ingredients. The nonnas can hear a recipe once and commit it to memory. But this woman does not understand the nonnas' tradition. Never share a whole recipe. She should leave out at least one ingredient.

As soon as the nonnas are out of earshot, they discuss their close encounter. "They don't seem so bad," Maddelana says. "And she did tell us about the stew."

"Yes, but she probably left something out," Concetta says.

"I'll try it," Maddelana says. "I'm going to the grocer's to buy paprika—hot and sweet."

That evening, the nonnas are on their way to church for their weekly novena. "I made the paprikash," Maddelana says. "I don't think she left out anything. It was delicious."

"Now if she would only fix those drapes." Concetta says.

BEEF PAPRIKASH

Serves six

3 tablespoons olive oil
1 cup diced celery
1 cup diced carrots
1 onion, diced
2 garlic cloves, quartered
3 tablespoons sweet paprika
1 to 2 tablespoons hot paprika
½ teaspoon dried oregano
1 bay leaf
Salt
Freshly ground pepper
1 tablespoon tomato paste
2 tablespoons flour
1 cup dry wine, red or white
1 ½ to 2 cups boiling water
2 pounds beef bottom round, rump, or chuck, cut into 2-inch cubes

Preheat oven to 325 degrees F.

In a nonreactive casserole, warm 2 tablespoons oil. Add vegetables, herbs, spices, and salt and pepper to taste.

Sauté about 15 minutes, or until golden.

Add tomato paste; sauté 5 minutes. Add flour; sauté over low heat 5 minutes.

Heat remaining tablespoon olive oil in large skillet.

Dry beef well; sprinkle with salt and pepper.

Brown beef on all sides in skillet; do not crowd; add browned beef to casserole.

Deglaze skillet with wine; add water; bring liquids to boil; pour over ingredients in casserole.

Stir well; liquid should barely cover meat. Add more water if necessary; bring to boil.

Cover casserole; place in lower third of oven; cook $1\frac{1}{2}$ to 2 hours, or until meat is fork-tender.

Serve over noodles.

Anything for Thanksgiving?

One of the nonnas' greatest joys on Thanksgiving morning is to dress the grandchildren in ragamuffin outfits for their run around the neighborhood begging for coins, candy, crayons, or just "anything for Thanksgiving." Concetta, Aniella, Maddelana, and Giuseppina take the old custom seriously and try to outdo one another in devising costumes. They compete over creating costumes almost more than they compete over cooking.

Concetta is draping Calogero's old oversize double-breasted suit jacket on a grandson. "You're almost ready," she says, sticking a DeNobili cigar in the jacket pocket.

In the meantime, Aniella wraps a clothesline belt around a pair of huge pink flannel pajama pants that her granddaughter wears. "Hold still," she says as she places a furry felt fedora on the girl's head.

But Giuseppina doesn't stop with just a costume. She holds a lighted match to a cork from a wine bottle. When the cork is charred, she blows out the flame, waits for it to cool, and uses the char to paint a mustache and goatee on her grandson. "*Bello, bello*," she cries. With that, the boy picks up a pillowcase to hold his loot and runs down the stairs and outside to join his buddies in their quest for Thanksgiving treats.

Aniella is happy not to have the children underfoot, as the oven heat from a roasting turkey coats her windows with droplets of moisture. The turkey is only one third of the main courses. There is lasagna with a variety of gravy meats and roast beef for those who cannot abide the traditional bird.

In her kitchen, Concetta is busy preparing appetizers. She stuffs giant mushrooms, gloating over the fact that the mushrooms she is filling with parsley, bread crumbs, and oil are surely twice as big as those of Maddelana.

On this American holiday, the nonnas also serve an American appetizer. They fill small glass oval plates (won in skeet ball games at Coney Island) with canned black olives, carrot sticks, and celery sticks and place them on the coffee table. On the dining table, they display slices of crisp fennel with fronds attached, split Cerignola olives sprinkled with olive oil and red pepper flakes, and a mixed *giardinera* salad bursting with pickled carrots, cauliflower, and pearl onions.

Calogero and his friends have been waiting on line since before 7am at the baker's for the bread and pastries. The line is moving too slowly for Maddelana as she passes on her way home from church. In two minutes, she assembles the group into two lines. "Who is waiting to pick up an order?" she shouts. "Stand over here, please." Then she commands, "If you're waiting to place an order, get in this line." She marches into the shop triumphantly and explains her scheme to the baker. As she leaves the store, she calls to the baker, "Some hot coffee for them would be nice." She modestly dismisses the group's thanks with a wave of her hand and starts for home again.

The guests and the children converge on Concetta's house at noon. Dinner is at two. In the meantime, they snack on prosciutto, mozzarella, roast peppers, and anchovies served on a pizza-size platter. The crusty bread overflows its basket next to the platter. Grown-ups sip glasses of red wine; the children guzzle cream soda mixed with a touch of wine.

Aniella stops by to borrow some folding chairs. Concetta insists that Aniella take a taste of the stuffing she has baked.

"Very good," Aniella says. "I taste the sausage. But in mine, this year, I put sausage *and* chestnuts."

Not to be outdone by Aniella wielding the folding chairs, Concetta, at the stove, shakes a tin of chestnuts, slashed and ready for the oven. "I'm serving chestnuts, two pounds of them, after dinner," she says. "Everybody can have *more* of them than they would in stuffing."

STUFFED MUSHROOMS

Serves six

24 large mushrooms, stems removed, tips of stems discarded
3 garlic cloves, finely minced
$\frac{1}{4}$ cup flat-leaf parsley, finely minced
$\frac{1}{2}$ cup fresh bread crumbs
6 tablespoons olive oil
Salt
Freshly ground pepper

Preheat oven to 425 degrees F.

Finely dice mushroom stems.

Mix together mushroom stems, garlic, parsley, and bread crumbs.

Blend in 4 tablespoons olive oil; add salt and pepper to taste.

Place remaining 2 tablespoons olive oil in a shallow casserole.

Add a pinch of salt to oil in casserole.

Toss mushroom caps in casserole until they are covered with oil.

Arrange caps in one layer in casserole.

Fill each cap generously with filling.

Bake 15 to 20 minutes, or until caps and filling are golden brown.

Serve warm or at room temperature.

WINTER

Let the Season Start

Once Thanksgiving is past, Concetta, Aniella, Giuseppina, and Maddelana believe that winter has arrived. To them, Thanksgiving is the beginning of the holiday season. With that in mind, on the morning after Thanksgiving, they scurry to the homes of grandchildren, ringing front doorbells until the children appear. No child is late. The nonnas, with their charges in tow, meet on the corner near the church.

Little children holding hands with nonnas, older children holding hands with one another, they all race down the avenue to the local five-and-ten-cent store. When they arrive, they see the crowd is being shepherded into one line. But no one complains.

At 9:30, the doors to the store open and the nonnas and children begin a climb to the second floor. As they reach the top step, they smile and hold the children close.

"It's more beautiful than it was last year," Maddelana says to her grandson.

"Look, they have silver bells hanging above the chair," Giuseppina says to her granddaughter.

Sitting in the chair amid the glory of a winter wonderland is Santa Claus. The nonnas try not to show they are as excited as the grandchildren. But Concetta gets caught up in admiring the tinsel showered everywhere. She turns to Maddelana. "Remember when the War was on and we had to save the tinsel every year?"

"I hated that job, wrapping all that silver stuff around a piece of cardboard," Maddelana says. "But look how much is here with all the blue ornaments decorating the tree. That's so different."

"Phew, the tree is artificial," Giuseppina scoffs. "I still like ornaments of all colors, not just blue, on a real tree."

"Oh," Maddelana says, "there's those little cardboard houses with the shiny snow on the roofs, under the tree. Just like the ones we have at home. So pretty."

"Look at the big bright Merry Christmas sign," Aniella says. She points to a die-cut sign glowing with silver glitter.

Now the line to sit on Santa's lap is moving quickly. Concetta bends down and whispers to her granddaughter, "Tell Santa what you want," knowing she will purchase whatever the child asks for. She remains within earshot, a tear or two of joy running down her cheek as the girl shares her list.

When the last grandchild climbs off Santa's lap, the children and the nonnas return to the first floor. It's time for a snack.

On this special day, the children can have anything they want. The nonnas grant all their wishes. Giuseppina purchases loose potato chips from a glass-enclosed counter. Aniella indulges her grandchildren with crisp hot waffles filled with melting ice cream from the snack bar.

Maddelana's grandchildren pull her to the candy counter and beg for a pound of carnival-colored jujubes. But Concetta shakes her head and passes up the cookies. "We bake better ones, the angeletti, at home," she tells her granddaughter, unwrapping a giant chocolate bar for the child.

The group walks the aisles in the store. The nonnas look at scarves, hats, and gloves, mentioning the names of sons-in-law who would enjoy such gifts.

Their daughters and grandchildren receive handmade gifts—a robe that Concetta "runs up" in what she claims takes 20 minutes but actually takes three days. Maddelana strings iridescent beads for necklaces for her daughters' gifts. Aniella knits scarves and mittens for her daughter and granddaughters. And Giuseppina, even though her "hands are killing" her (as usual), crochets a bed jacket for her daughter.

In the Christmas department, the children select a few ornaments to take home. Soon the nonnas are paying for bright red glass bells topped with sugary-looking "snow."

Across from the ornament display is a counter covered with artificial green turf. It is home to a miniature stable for a *presepio*, or Christmas crib. The stable holds plaster figurines of the Holy Family surrounded by a variety of plaster barnyard animals, several shepherds with crooks, and three kings bearing gifts.

Concetta picks up a plaster lamb. "This maybe won't go with the set I got from my mother, but you can never have too many animals to keep the Baby Jesus warm."

That is all it takes for the others to decide they cannot be outdone in making a comfortable home for the Baby Jesus.

There is an immediate run on cows and goats and sheep and even a camel, part of the Three Kings entourage. Concetta, Maddelana, Giuseppina, and Aniella are each determined to keep their Holy Family warmest with the breath of animals.

ANGELETTI—LEMON-ICED COOKIES

Makes 48 cookies

$2\frac{1}{4}$ cups all-purpose flour
1 tablespoon baking powder
$\frac{1}{4}$ teaspoon salt
$\frac{1}{2}$ cup (1 stick) unsalted butter at room temperature
$\frac{1}{2}$ cup granulated sugar
3 large eggs
1 teaspoon vanilla

ICING
3 cups confectioners' sugar
Grated rind of 1 lemon
2 to 3 tablespoons lemon juice
Colored sprinkles (optional)

Preheat oven to 350 degrees F.

Sift together flour, salt, and baking powder; set aside.

In the bowl of an electric mixer fitted with a paddle attachment, cream butter and granulated sugar until fluffy.

Add eggs one at a time; beat well after each addition; beat in vanilla.

With mixer on, gradually add flour mixture; beat until dough comes together.

Gently roll bits of dough into 1 to $1\frac{1}{2}$ inch balls and place on lightly buttered or parchment-lined baking sheets.

Bake until golden, 15 to 18 minutes. Transfer cookies to wire cooling rack set over a sheet of waxed paper.

In a medium bowl, stir together confectioners' sugar, lemon rind, and lemon juice to form a smooth glossy icing.

When cookies are cool, dip tops in icing and return to wire rack.

Shower with colored sprinkles if desired; leave on wire cooling rack until icing is firm.

Celebrating a Saint

On a blustery Friday night in December, Concetta's and Giuseppina's husbands, together with two friends from the neighborhood, walk up the stairs of Concetta's tenement. They stop to knock at the door on each landing as they make their way to the top floor. Each family greets them, offers them anisette or wine (always accepted) or an espresso (often declined), and gives them money.

They are not loan sharks or bookies coming to collect their take. They are members of a committee asking for donations for a springtime feast for the saint. Not *a* saint, but *the* saint—Saint Michael, Saint Anne, Our Lady of Mount Carmel, Saint Anthony, among others—the patron of their *paese* in the old country.

There are as many committees as there are patron saints. The men don't expect a windfall, just small donations that allow them to carry on the tradition. Most people give only change, so when the collectors receive a dollar, it's a big deal. The committee members look forward to ordering the lights, hiring the entertainers, and assisting with the parade. They also anticipate going out of an evening (or several) to enjoy the hospitality of their neighbors, raise some funds, and return home in a far happier mood than when they left.

As they approach Concetta's door, she looks annoyed and turns to Giuseppina. "I don't know why they have to keep up this collecting!"

"I agree," says Giuseppina, lighting up a Chesterfield. "Even for a saint's feast. I told my daughter just to give them some change and not make them comfortable at the table. If you do, they expect some anisette."

"And who knows what shape they'll be in when they come home—with a drop of anisette here, a drop of Marsala there," Concetta pauses. "Put out that cigarette, my little grandson is sleeping in the bedroom."

Giuseppina, stubbing out the cigarette, says, "Last year, one night my husband came home singing at the top of his lungs after he made a collection. I told him if he does it again, I'm not letting him in the house."

"I kept Calogero home one night; I did not let him go collecting," Concetta says. "But I felt bad."

Soon there is a knock at the door. The group, including Calogero, makes it past Concetta; she offers them no refreshments. She glares at her husband, who is sporting his committee pin on his worn work jacket. She makes a donation and accepts a large prayer card displaying a victorious Saint Michael driving a lance through a fallen angel.

The men rise to leave, and Giuseppina collars her husband. She gives him a stern look. "Remember, you got work tomorrow."

As the committee turns toward the door, a baby cries. In seconds, Concetta opens a French door separating the kitchen from the rest of the apartment. That's all it takes. Calogero, the glowing grandfather, cannot resist showing off his new grandson to the rest of the committee. The men ooh and aah and tell the baby that he is strong and beautiful. One of them traces a sign of the cross on the little one's forehead.

Even Giuseppina is overcome by the fuss the men make over the baby; she gets weepy. Concetta invites the men to sit in the kitchen. She places on the table a bottle of anisette and four miniature cordial mugs, rushes to the sink, and fills a *machinetta* with water for espresso. She hesitates for a moment, then goes to the cupboard—for a box of biscotti.

Concetta fills the glasses and offers a toast, "To our grandson, and to Saint Michael. And to a good, big collection this year."

BISCOTTI

Makes 12 slices

$1\frac{1}{4}$ cups all-purpose, unbleached flour

$\frac{1}{4}$ teaspoon salt

$\frac{1}{2}$ teaspoon baking powder

$\frac{2}{3}$ cup sugar

4 tablespoons unsalted butter plus 1 tablespoon, room temperature

2 large eggs

1 teaspoon pure vanilla extract

$\frac{1}{4}$ teaspoon almond extract

$\frac{3}{4}$ cup almonds, blanched, toasted

Preheat oven to 375 degrees F.

Coat a loaf pan with the 1 tablespoon butter; sprinkle with flour to coat.

Mix together flour, salt, and baking powder.

Cream remaining butter and sugar with vanilla and almond extract.

Beat eggs into butter mixture; mix in dry ingredients and almonds.

Spread mixture in pan.

Bake about 20 minutes, or until a toothpick inserted in center comes out clean.

Reduce oven temperature to 325 degrees F.

Remove "cake" from pan; place on wire cooling rack; cool; slice into 12 biscuits.

Place slices on parchment-lined baking sheet; return to oven.

Bake 6 minutes, or until slices are golden; turn slices; bake another 5 minutes.

Cool on wire rack.

Ready for a Wedding

It is late afternoon on a wintry Saturday; the sun is hiding behind a cloud. Concetta, Maddelana, and Aniella sit around Concetta's kitchen table. Each is crocheting a lacy gift for a June bride. Their fingers move nimbly to cast onto their crochet hooks the finest cotton thread—thin enough to sew seams on a silk wedding dress. There is no question of color here. They all use white or eggshell. Their job is to create individual spider-web-like flowers to join together into a bedspread, a tablecloth, doilies—and maybe runners for the dressers too.

A huge pot of chicken soup simmering on the stove adds mist to the windows and an appetite-teasing aroma to the kitchen. The women are working quietly when the door bursts open. Giuseppina stops in for a visit.

She takes off her coat and settles herself at the table. "What is that smell from the chicken soup?" she asks. "It's not bad," she says, wrinkling her nose. "But it is different."

Giuseppina has hit a nerve. The others begin to talk, sharing their opinion on the scent of the soup. "I didn't want to say anything," Aniella says. "It does smell delicious, but different. Maybe American? What did you put in it?"

"I went to buy carrots and celery, and the carrots were tied in a bunch with a parsnip and a turnip," Concetta says. "I asked Mike, the vegetable man, what the other vegetables were doing with the carrots. He said, 'Americans call this a bunch of soup greens.' They put it in soup."

Stirring the soup, she says, "So I try it. I'm making wedding soup and I want a nice rich broth."

"Ah, wedding soup, *minestra maritati*," Maddelana says, giggling. "And we're making wedding gifts."

"Bah, listen to her," Giuseppina says, lighting her first Chesterfield of the afternoon. Concetta scurries to her side and hands her a huge ashtray. "She thinks everything's funny."

"Besides," Maddelana says, "they call them soup greens, but there are no greens in them, just carrots and turnips. In wedding soup, you have to 'marry' the meat with real greens—escarole, spinach, or something like that."

"I know," says Concetta. "I bought a big bunch of escarole. And when the soup is ready, I'm adding that and the tiny meatballs."

The prickly Giuseppina has run out of steam. Instead of making another stinging remark to the nonnas she's been zinging for too many years to count, she sighs. "I love the soup mamma makes—not filled with just greens and meatballs, but with provolone, crusts of Parmigiano, bits of prosciutto, and sopressata."

And they're off. Each nonna adds another ingredient to the soup her mother used to make. A tureen as big as Naples could not hold all the meats, cheeses, greens, and broth they come up with. They end the list sounding as satisfied as if they had downed the entire dish.

"Tomorrow you all get a taste," Concetta says. "A wedding soup with an American touch."

"Save some for me," Giuseppina says, "even though it smells different."

WEDDING SOUP

Serves 8

CHICKEN SOUP
Two 3- to 4-pound chickens, quartered, excess fat removed
1 large onion, roughly sliced
3 large carrots, peeled, diced
4 stalks celery, diced
1 small parsnip, peeled, finely diced
1 small white turnip, peeled, finely diced
Salt and freshly ground pepper to taste

Place all ingredients except salt and pepper in a 6-quart pot.

Cover chicken and vegetables with cold water; bring to a boil, uncovered, on high heat.

Skim foam that rises to the top; reduce heat to simmer.

Add a generous amount of salt and pepper; partially cover pot; stir occasionally.

Simmer about 75 minute or until chicken is cooked through.

Remove chicken pieces from broth; skin and bone chicken.

Break meat into small pieces; place meat on platter, cover, and refrigerate.

Return bones and skin to soup; simmer uncovered, 2 hours; discard skin and bones.

Refrigerate soup up to 24 hours or until fat rises and hardens.

Remove congealed fat; reheat soup for serving or refrigerate.

Use within two days or freeze in small containers and use within a couple of weeks.

MEATBALLS AND GREENS
4 cups chicken soup defatted, skin and bones removed,
**   plus 4 additional cups**
1 pound ground sirloin
1 large egg
1 slice white bread, in pieces
3 tablespoons whole milk
1 garlic clove grated
6 tablespoons minced fresh flat-leaf parsley, divided
Salt and freshly ground pepper to taste
1 bunch escarole, well washed, thinly sliced
1½ cups diced reserved chicken from soup

Bring 4 cups chicken soup to simmer in a nonreactive pot.

In a large bowl, squeeze bread in milk; add 3 tablespoons parsley and remaining ingredients, except escarole.

Shape beef mixture into tiny balls.

Drop meatballs into simmering soup.

Skim and discard foam and fat that rises to surface of soup.

Simmer 10 minutes, or until meatballs are cooked through.

Add simmering soup and meatballs to the 4 additional cups of soup.

Add diced cooked chicken and reserved escarole to soup.

Simmer until escarole is wilted and soup is heated through.

Sprinkle with remaining 3 tablespoons parsley before serving.

Nonnas and the Red Menace

It's been a long, eventful and, what has turned out to be, blessed nine months. Now a little guy is happily ensconced in a well-upholstered bassinet in a second-floor apartment in Concetta's Brooklyn tenement. The visitors come daily. Other not-so-new mothers—sisters, cousins, and friends—arrive on a rotating schedule to burp, diaper, and bathe the new arrival, and to give the new mom a chance to rest.

It is only a matter of time before Concetta, Aniella, Maddelana, and Giuseppina visit. As they approach the apartment, Maddelana turns to Giuseppina, "Remember, no smoking when the baby is around."

Giuseppina rolls her eyes. "Of course, I know," she says as she expertly tosses a cigarette over the curb and into the street.

In the apartment, they deposit on the kitchen table's grey enamel surface an abundance of fruit, primarily huge navel oranges (for the mom to eat as Giuseppina says, "to get her strength back"). They also open a brown paper bag, and out spill boxes of spaghetti, linguini, and spaghettini, tins of oil-packed anchovies, bunches of parsley, heads of garlic, and bags of breadcrumbs from the local *panettiere*.

"A little something to keep in the house," Concetta says.

"In case you can't get to the store," Maddelana says, "you can make *pasta alici*, pasta with anchovies."

Aniella triumphantly places a box tied with red and white bakery string on the table. "Some regina for you," she says of the contents. The regina? That omnipresent sesame-seeded cookie that must accompany a cup of coffee. The implication? Of course, the nonnas will stay for coffee.

And then they approach the bassinet. Concetta makes a sign of the cross on the little one's forehead, then kisses her fingers and points her eyes heavenward—all the while watching for the reaction of the others, to make sure they realize that hers is the most elaborate blessing. Each in turn holds the little guy, squeezing his tiny feet, clasping his baby fingers, and saying, "Such long fingers; he's going to play the piano." There's no rest for the new mom now; she bustles about making coffee, setting out plates of cookies, and answering questions about the upcoming christening.

"When?" Concetta asks.

"Where?" inquires Maddelana.

And Giuseppina voices the most important question—"Who?" She is of course referring to the prospective godparents. The parents must assign them according to some very specific rules in order to "keep the peace." The nonnas approve the mom's decision and then approach a most delicate topic, the real reason for their visit.

They set their smiles and begin.

"The baby has a beautiful bassinet, such pretty colors—all blue, and white, and yellow," Concetta says.

Aniella picks up; she knows the drill. "Maybe there should be a little something red though, no?" she asks quietly. "

"A little something red—even just a ribbon—you know, to ward off the *mal'occhio*," says Maddelana.

At the mention of the evil eye, the new mom is noncommittal. She says, "We'll think about it."

The nonnas prepare to say their good-byes. Concetta stops at the bassinet to kiss the baby while she digs her hand into the pocket of her front apron and goes through a sort of gyration. Giuseppina bends as if to pick something up off the floor. Aniella seems to be realigning the top of the mattress, lifting it ever so slightly. Maddelana carefully adjusts the ruffled organdy that covers the hood of the bassinet.

They say their farewells to the new mom and leave.

Several hours later, the mom strips the bassinet to put the sheets and coverings in the wash. She finds four small gold-colored safety pins attached to four tiny red ribbons, one under the skirt, one on the sheet, one beneath the mattress, and one hidden under a ruffle on the hood cover.

The nonnas are never denied their right to defeat the *mal'occhio*.

PASTA WITH ANCHOVIES

Serves four

1 pound pasta (spaghetti, thin linguine—any long, thin pasta)
2 cloves garlic, quartered
2 small tins anchovies packed in olive oil
¼ cup olive oil
6 tablespoons fresh bread crumbs, toasted
Salt and freshly ground pepper
Dash red pepper flakes (optional)
3 tablespoons, flat-leaf Italian parsley, minced

Bring 5 quarts of lightly salted (anchovies are salty) water to a boil in a covered pot.

In a wide, shallow skillet, sauté the garlic until golden with a little bit of salt and pepper.

Remove garlic and discard.

Add the anchovies with their oil to the garlic-infused oil.

Simmer slowly until the anchovies dissolve; stir in the capers and the breadcrumbs.

Toss the pasta into the rapidly boiling water and stir.

Test pasta for doneness (after 8 to 10 minutes); drain and fold it into the sauce.

Over medium heat, shake the pan until the pasta is coated with sauce.

Sprinkle pasta with parsley; serve.

Queen of the Transfers

It is a Friday afternoon and Concetta, Aniella, and Giuseppina are cleaning the church. The door opens, letting in a burst of winter air as Maddelana, a late arrival, enters. Under her heavy coat, she wears an outfit much like that of the others—black dress, a colorful front apron. But she has accessorized her costume with a necklace. No ordinary necklace, it is a string of rosary beads.

Maddelana is an inveterate churchgoer: morning, noon, and night. Distance is no object when she decides to make a novena in Manhattan, attend a funeral Mass in Brooklyn, and show up for a blessing by a visiting Neapolitan bishop in the Bronx—all on the same day. She gets around via subway and trolley by wielding her secret weapon, a New York City transit transfer.

Rifling through her pocketbook, she settles herself in a pew and smiles triumphantly as she fans out a series of transfers like a hand of cards. "This one is finished at six o'clock," Maddelana says, separating one transfer from the bunch. "So I have to catch a trolley at a quarter to six to be on time for this novena I'm making."

The others nod and roll their eyes at her announcement as she continues to identify each transfer and the amount of life it has left in it. "This one is good until noon tomorrow," she says. "I'll use it to take the trolley to the subway and go to Mass at the church near Macy's." Satisfied, she clasps her pocketbook shut. "After the church on 33rd Street, I have to go to downtown Brooklyn to help clean the church there."

Besides being the thriftiest among them, she is also either the most naïve or the most insensitive. "Giuseppina," she addresses her sister, "Mamma is putting up some fresh *baccala*; you know, codfish in sauce, so I don't have to cook tonight."

She constantly reminds the others that she and Giuseppina are the last among them to have a living mother—a 90-year-old—who sits in the window of her third floor apartment, patiently waiting for Maddelana to finish her steeple chase.

The nonnas take her behavior in stride. They know she has had heartache, and her churchgoing is one of the results. Maddelana is a bit older than the others. Her husband served in France in World War I and returned home suffering from shell shock. He does not join the men in collecting for a saint or go to their apartments to share an anisette or play a game of *brisc*.

"Okay, enough talking," Concetta says briskly. "It's your turn to iron the altar cloth. The ironing board is in the sacristy. "

The rosary beads tinkle lightly as Maddelana makes her way to the front of the church.

"Oh, and don't forget," Aniella calls after her. "Coffee and cake at my house tonight—after your novena."

The sisterhood remains united.

CODFISH IN TOMATO SAUCE

Serves four

4 tablespoons olive oil
Sprinkle red pepper flakes
Salt and freshly ground pepper to taste
½ cup diced onion
¼ teaspoon fennel seeds
½ teaspoon dried basil (or 1 tablespoon fresh, minced)
Pinch saffron (optional)
1 dried bay leaf
1 cup tomato sauce, store-bought or homemade
4 tablespoons anisette or Pernod
¼ cup vermouth
2 pounds fresh cod or scrod, well washed, dried

In a heavy, wide nonreactive skillet, gently heat oil, salt, and peppers.

Add onions; sauté until golden.

Raise heat to high, then turn off.

Add anisette, vermouth, and herbs; raise heat to low; stir.

Simmer over low heat until alcohol burns off and reduces by half.

Add tomato sauce; simmer on medium heat until sauce thickens and coats a spoon.

Add fish; bring to a boil; reduce heat to medium.

Partially cover skillet; cook fish 14 to 16 minutes, or until it flakes easily with a fork.

Serve with crusty Italian or French bread

The Christmas Eve Feast

It doesn't matter where Concetta, Giuseppina, Maddelana, and Anniela were born. On Christmas Eve, they serve the same dishes in South Brooklyn as their families served in Naples or Sicily or Calabria. The mouthwatering aroma of fish anointed with garlic and olive oil, capers, raisins, and crispy crunchy crust fills the whole neighborhood as the nonnas and their families prepare not just a dinner but a *Vigilia*.

The traditional vigil takes place while they await the birth of the Bambino Gesu. Before the midnight church service, before the opening of the gifts, before the placing of a tiny Jesus statue in a manger under the tree, but after the tree-trimming and the shopping marathon ends, the relatives and guests arrive, and the feasting begins.

Concetta, Maddelana, Giuseppina, and Aniella and their families live in neighborhoods where other people from their hometowns—on the other side—live. So the cooking of a particular region lives on in different parts of Brooklyn. And therein lies the tiniest bit of friction in what is otherwise a joyous holiday. The one thing the dishes have in common is fish—and lots of it. But Maddelana, Concetta, and Giuseppina, with roots in Naples and Calabria, elect to cook a different seven-fishes feast from the one Aniella prepares. Aniella still has relatives in Sicily. In the days leading up to the Eve, the nonnas meet most often at the fish market.

"Sardines, sardines, nice fresh ones, please," shouts Aniella to make sure the fishmonger hears her.

"Oh, fa!" says Giuseppina, in what is a quiet voice for her. "Sardines? Doesn't she know about anchovies in olive oil? Or whiting, *merluzzo*? I know she knows shrimp and dried cod, *baccala*." She shakes her head in disbelief and turns to Concetta. "And sardines, they're so boney, no matter how you cook them. Bah!" Giuseppina catches the eye of the fishmonger and requests, "Three pounds of *merluzzo*, please."

Overhearing this exchange, Aniella pipes up. "So, you'll use anchovies in the pasta, not sardines?" She answers her own question sharply. "Because sardines are too tough to clean. Eh, whiting and anchovies, they're lazy people's food."

"No, they're not," says Concetta as she points out her choice merluzzo to the fishmonger. "They're holiday food; that's why they're special."

"My mother still keeps cooking them just the way her mother did in Italy," Maddelana says, always eager to remind them her mother is still up and about.

And soon each is telling a tale of Mamma—her mamma—and her Christmas Eve exploits. They laugh at some of the stories, nod their heads knowingly, and dab at their eyes as they reminisce.

"They really knew how to celebrate," Concetta says, "and they had nothing. We have everything, and we argue about anchovies."

The subject is closed, the bickering forgotten. "We meet on the corner at 7:30 tonight to walk to church for the novena."

SICILIAN PASTA WITH SARDINES

Serves eight

2 pounds sardines, boned, rinsed well, dried
2 bunches fennel
1 onion, chopped
$\frac{1}{2}$ cup olive oil
$\frac{1}{4}$ cup pine nuts
$\frac{1}{2}$ cup dried currants (soaked 5 minutes in hot water to cover)
$\frac{1}{2}$ cup toasted almonds
8 anchovy fillets
Salt and freshly ground pepper to taste
1$\frac{1}{2}$ pounds bucatini or perciatelli
2 cups toasted fresh white bread crumbs

Trim the fennel of some of its fronds, wash well, core, slice thinly.

Boil fennel—in the 5 quarts of salted water that you will use to boil the pasta—10 minutes or until it is tender.

In a large shallow skillet, heat $\frac{1}{4}$ cup olive oil; add onions, nuts, drained currants, almonds, and anchovies; sauté until onions turn golden; sprinkle with salt and pepper.

Set ingredients aside; wipe out skillet.

Sauté sardines until golden in remaining $\frac{1}{4}$ cup oil

Remove sardines from pan; add fennel and stir to coat with oil; sprinkle with salt and pepper; stir nut mixture into fennel

Boil pasta in fennel water until cooked to your liking; drain pasta.

Toss pasta into fennel mixture; warm over medium heat until pasta absorbs sauce.

Carefully fold in sardines.

Top with toasted bread crumbs; serve.

NEAPOLITAN PASTA

Serves six

2 jars best-quality anchovy fillets, packed in olive oil
2 tablespoons capers, rinsed and diced
3 cloves garlic, quartered
½ cup olive oil
2 tablespoons pine nuts, toasted
½ cup fresh bread crumbs ground from good quality white bread
2 tablespoons chopped Italian flat-leaf parsley
1 pound farfalle or bucatini

Put 5 quarts salted water on to boil for pasta.

While pasta is boiling, in a skillet heat olive oil until it shimmers.

Add garlic and cook until it is golden; add anchovies with their oil.
Stir rapidly to break up anchovies; reduce heat.

Stir in bread crumbs, pine nuts, and parsley; toss in pasta; heat until
pasta is covered with sauce; serve.

NEAPOLITAN BACCALA

Serves six

Purchase dried cod several days in advance to allow time to soak it.

$1\frac{1}{2}$ **pounds dried cod soaked until free of salt**
1 large white onion diced
$\frac{1}{4}$ **cup olive oil**
3 tablespoons anisette or pernod
$\frac{1}{4}$ **cup dry white wine or vermouth**
Pinch of salt
Sprinkle fennel seeds
Freshly ground pepper
Red pepper flakes to taste
Bay leaf
1 can San Marzano tomatoes

Two days before serving: Place fish in a large bowl of cold water in the refrigerator. Rinse fish and change water every 4 hours, or as often as possible.

On serving day: In a heavy nonreactive pot, sauté the onion in oil; add spices.

Reduce heat and carefully add wine and anisette.

Over a low flame, allow alcohol to evaporate; stir in tomatoes.

Simmer sauce until thickened and reduced by half—about 30 minutes.

Slice baccala into 4-inch pieces; add to sauce.

Simmer 15–20 minutes or until fish flakes easily; serve.

SICILIAN BACCALA

Serves six

Follow previous recipe for sauce.

Before adding tomatoes to sauce, add $\frac{1}{4}$ cup toasted pine nuts and $\frac{1}{2}$ cup currants to the sauce.

When fish is ready, stir 2 cubed boiled potatoes into sauce.

FRITTO MISTO (POPULAR ALL OVER)

Serves 12

$1\frac{1}{2}$ **pounds baccala, soaked and dried**
3 pounds calamari, sliced into rings, tentacles left whole
$1\frac{1}{2}$ **pounds whiting (*merluzzo*) fillets, skin left on, rinsed, dried**
2 pounds large shrimp, deveined, rinsed, dried
2 pounds sea scallops, rinsed, dried
2 pounds lemon sole or flounder fillets, rinsed, dried
3 cups all-purpose flour
2 to 4 cups olive oil (NOT extra-virgin)
Coarse salt to taste
4 lemons sliced in quarters

Wash and dry fish.

Heat two large frying pans, preferably nonstick; place two large cookie sheets with rims (jelly-roll pans) in a 170 degree F. oven.

Add enough oil to completely cover the bottoms of the frying pans with a layer about $\frac{1}{8}$-inch thick.

Place the flour in a paper lunch bag.

While frying pans are heating, begin to add a few pieces of fish at a time to the flour. Shake each piece to remove excess flour.

Fry fish in hot oil, making sure there is enough room between pieces to ensure even browning.

Place fried fish on baking sheets in oven.

Add more oil as needed to pans.

If flour forms a heavy coating in pan, wipe out pan, add fresh oil, and start again.

Salt right before serving with lemon slices.

NEAPOLITAN FISH SALAD

Serves four

Early in day: Select one of the fried fishes above, not the seafood; fry according to recipe above.

1 pound fried fish
¼ teaspoon red pepper flakes
6 thinly sliced onion rings
1 tablespoon red wine vinegar
Salt to taste

Place fish in a single layer on platter.

Sprinkle with remaining ingredients.

Serve at room temperature.

SICILIAN MUSSELS

Serves four

4 pounds cultivated mussels, clean, debearded
6 cloves garlic quartered
½ cup olive oil
Freshly grated pepper
Pinch salt
4 tablespoons anisette
1 cup dry vermouth
¼ cup chopped flat-leaf Italian parsley

Dash of salt and freshly ground pepper to taste

Scrub and debeard mussels.

In a deep nonreactive frying pan, sauté garlic in olive oil; add salt and pepper, wine, and anisette. Reduce wine and anisette.

Add mussels; cover pan closely; shake pan occasionally until mussels open, about 7 to 10 minutes; discard any that do not open.

Serve with toasted country bread slices to sop up sauce.

NEAPOLITAN BAKED RED SNAPPER

Serves four

1 whole red snapper, slit down one side, cleaned, gutted, head removed, washed and dried
1 large diced onion
$\frac{1}{4}$ cup olive oil plus 2 tablespoons
$\frac{1}{2}$ cup freshly made toasted bread cubes from good quality white bread
Salt
Freshly ground pepper
$\frac{1}{4}$ pound large shrimp, cleaned, deveined, washed, dried and diced
3 tablespoons anisette
3 tablespoons white wine plus 3 additional tablespoons

Preheat oven to 425 degrees F.

Rub fish all over with some of the $\frac{1}{4}$ cup oil.

Coat a large nonreactive baking dish with 1 tablespoon oil.

Heat the remaining oil in a frying pan; sauté the diced onion until it is slightly golden and translucent; add salt, pepper, bread cubes; stir until cubes begin to turn pale gold.

Increase heat, add shrimp; sauté shrimp until cooked through.

Add anisette, 3 tablespoons wine; stir; remove from heat.

Stuff cavity of red snapper with mixture; hold fish closed with toothpicks, skewers, or butcher's twine.

Sprinkle remaining 2 tablespoons oil and 3 tablespoons wine over and around fish.

Bake 25 to 30 minutes, or until fish flakes easily and skin is golden.

LIVORNESE PASTA WITH CLAM SAUCE

Serves six

4 dozen littleneck clams, well-scrubbed
$\frac{1}{2}$ cup olive oil
4 cloves garlic, quartered
6 tablespoons anisette
$\frac{1}{2}$ cup vermouth
Grated rind of one lemon
Juice of one lemon
Salt
Red pepper flakes
Chopped fresh flat-leaf parsley
$1\frac{1}{2}$ pounds thin linguine

In a large frying pan (with a lid), sauté garlic until golden in olive oil.

Turn off heat; carefully add anisette, and vermouth; reduce on low flame.

Add lemon rind and juice, salt and pepper flakes.

Raise heat to high; add clams; cover; cook about 7 to 10 minutes and check to see if clams are open.

Remove clams as they open; discard any clams that do not open.

Remove clams from shells; dice; return clams to sauce in skillet.

To 5 quarts boiling water, boil linguine to desired doneness; drain.

Add to clams and juice in skillet; toss over medium heat until pasta is covered with sauce; top with parsley; serve.

CALABRESE CALAMARI

Serves six

3 pounds squid, bodies sliced into $\frac{1}{4}$-inch rings;
  tentacles left whole
$\frac{1}{2}$ cup olive oil
1 large onion, diced
$\frac{1}{2}$ teaspoon salt
Freshly ground pepper to taste
2 cloves garlic, minced
1 can San Marzano tomatoes
1 cup red wine
1 tablespoon capers, rinsed
8 Gaeta olives, pitted, crushed
Red pepper flakes
1 teaspoon basil dried, 1 tablespoon fresh, minced
1 pound fusilli

In large nonreactive sauce pan, heat oil; add onions, garlic, salt, and pepper; sauté until onions are golden.

Add red wine, reduce by half.

Add tomatoes, capers, olives, red pepper, and basil.

Simmer for 15 to 20 minutes, or until sauce thickens.

Raise heat to high; bring sauce to a boil; add washed and dried squid; stir; return to boil.

Lower heat; partially cover pan; simmer 75 minutes, or until squid is fork-tender.

Add 2 tablespoons salt to 5 quarts of water; bring to boil; add fusilli; cook until al dente.

Drain pasta well; add to tender calamari; toss; simmer 5 minutes; serve.

SICILIAN ESCAROLE PIE

Serves six

CRUST

2 pounds pizza dough, store-bought or homemade

FILLING

2 cloves garlic, thinly sliced

½ cup plus 2 tablespoons olive oil

1 head escarole, washed, chopped, steamed 3 minutes

½ pound mozzarella diced

3 anchovy fillets cut in pieces

Salt

Freshly ground pepper.

Preheat oven to 400 degrees F.

Divide dough in half.

Oil a 9-inch pie pan with 1 tablespoon olive oil; line the pan with half the dough, leaving a slight overhang; trim excess dough.

In a frying pan, sauté garlic until golden

In a kitchen towel, squeeze as much water as possible out of escarole.

In the skillet, combine escarole with remaining ingredients.

Fill pie shell; roll out remaining dough; place crust on top, sealing it to bottom crust.

Pierce top crust with a knife.

Brush top crust with remaining tablespoon olive oil.

Place pie on baking sheet; bake 20 minutes, or until golden brown.

Cool on wire cooling rack; serve warm or at room temperature; refrigerate leftovers.

NEAPOLITAN SPINACH PIE

Serves six

2 pounds pizza dough, store-bought or homemade
Crushed red pepper to taste
$\frac{1}{4}$ cup olive oil plus 1 tablespoon
1 pound spinach, chopped, steamed, squeezed dry
1 pound ricotta
$\frac{1}{2}$ pound mozzarella diced
2 eggs, beaten
Salt and pepper to taste
$\frac{1}{2}$ cup grated Parmesan

Preheat oven to 400 degrees F.

Divide the dough in half.

Oil a 9-inch pie pan with a bit of the olive oil.

Line the pan with half the dough, leaving a slight overhang;
trim excess.

Set aside 1 tablespoon olive oil to brush top crust.

Combine all remaining ingredients.

Fill pie shell; place crust on top, sealing it to bottom crust.

Brush top crust with olive oil

Pierce top crust with a knife.

Place pie on baking sheet; bake 20 minutes or until golden brown.

Cool on wire cooling rack; serve warm or at room temperature;
refrigerate leftovers.

A Baby Is Born

On Christmas Eve, Concetta, Aniella, Maddelana, and Giuseppina meet on the corner near the church. They are on their way to Midnight Mass. "How did the baccala come out?" Maddelana asks Concetta. The others continue talking nonstop about their *Vigilia*, the Christmas Eve feast. Concetta says, "Oh, it was delicious—just right, not too many bones, and so rich. I made it *mantecata*; I must have used two cups of cream. Everybody loved it."

"Mine was so tasty, too," Aniella says. "I fixed it with tomato sauce, currants, and potatoes."

"Seven fishes, I made," Giuseppina says wearily. "Phew, you know how much I hate to cook. I probably made eight side dishes."

"After I finished frying the struffole and the zeppole, I baked the pannetone," Maddelana says.

Struffole. Panettone. Zeppole. Baccala. The words continue to surround them as they walk down the block. By the time they reach the church, they are out of breath. They genuflect hastily and cross themselves. Ready for the caroling that is to begin, they settle in "their" pew.

The scent of pine decorating the altar mingles with the scent of incense as the organ begins and the horns—special for this one night only—join in. The nonnas listen to "O Little Town of Bethlehem." Their granddaughters sing in the choir; Concetta strains to hear the voice of her particular 16-year-old. Maddelana raises her hand in a salute to her grandson, an altar boy, arrayed in miniature vestments.

They hum along to "The First Noel" and raise their voices to "Noel, Noel." Maddelana and Concetta glance at their wristwatches. Giuseppina looks at the lapel watch adorning the collar of her black coat; they are all ever more eager for midnight to arrive. It is at that moment, after the pastor places the Babe in the manger, their holiday truly begins. It is their once-a-year day. Soon, soon, they know it is approaching as they sit through the choir's soprano soloist singing "O Holy Night."

Now, to the strains of "Angels We Have Heard on High," the procession from the main altar begins. The nonnas rise to watch the Italian pastor and the two Irish curates make their way to the back of the church into the vestibule. The oldest and tallest altar boy, the thurifer, walking backward in front of them, gently swings a censer filling the air with a "this is church" aroma. The altar boys follow the priests. Maddelana winks at her grandson.

When the procession passes, the nonnas look in anticipation at the side altar where the empty manger rests, carved almost life-size in the Neapolitan fashion. Mary and Joseph, gazing on either side of the straw-filled cradle, are surrounded by fronds of pine where oxen and sheep nuzzle.

In minutes it is midnight. *"Adeste fideles* . . . Oh, come all ye faithful, joyful, and triumphant," trumpets loudly from the choir loft; the bells peal, and the nonnas sing exultantly *"Venite adoremus. . .* Oh, come let us adore Him, oh, come let us adore Him." The procession makes its way toward the altar. Swaddled in the pastor's vestments is a figure, a lifelike baby, the baby Jesus. A single tear slides down Concetta's cheek as the procession passes.

The pastor gently places the Babe in the manger. The organ and the horns accompany the choir as it begins to sing softly, *"Tu Scendi dalle Stella. . . .* You came down from a star." Concetta, Maddelana, Aniella, and Giuseppina clasp hands as they sing the centuries-old carol, their knuckles white from the pressure each is exerting on the hands of the other. It is the one time of year they hear and sing a hymn in their mother tongue.

Now their faces glisten with tears. It is Christmas Eve in Brooklyn. But for some of them it is Christmas Eve in a town they haven't seen in more than half a lifetime. They are children again at home.

"Buon Natale," they whisper to one another as the music ends.

BACCALA MANTECATO—DRIED COD PUREE

Serves eight

2 pounds dried cod, baccala (soaked in refrigerator for at least 2 days, with water changed 3 or 4 times a day)

4 Idaho or russet potatoes, peeled, sliced
2 bay leaves
½ cup dry vermouth
12 peppercorns
10 garlic cloves, peeled, sliced
1 to 2 cups olive oil (does not have to be virgin olive oil)
1 to 2 cups heavy cream
3 to 4 tablespoons fresh breadcrumbs
French bread croutons, baked until golden

Preheat oven to 375 degrees F.

Place potatoes in a large pot; add cold water to cover; add pinch of salt.

Cover pot; boil potatoes over high heat until very tender; drain.

Place potatoes back in pot; shake over medium heat until potatoes are dry.

Place vermouth, peppercorns, and bay leaf in a shallow pan; add fish.

Add enough water to barely cover fish; place pan on medium heat; bring to simmer.

Partially cover pan; poach 16 to 18 minutes, or until fish flakes easily.

In another frying pan over very low heat, sauté garlic in 1 cup olive oil with a pinch of salt for 20 minutes, or until garlic is golden brown.

In small saucepan, warm cream over very low heat.

Rice or mash potatoes in the hot pot in which they cooked; work in all but 2 tablespoons of olive oil and garlic (add additional oil if mixture isn't creamy enough).

Stir in flaked fish. Add warmed cream to taste.

Spread mixture in heatproof casserole; sprinkle with crumbs, reserved oil, and garlic.

Bake about 25 minutes; serve with baked croutons.

Happy New Year

The tenement basement with its laundry room, wine-making equipment, and ages-old sink and stove becomes a ballroom on New Year's Eve. Twisted colorful crepe-paper streamers criss-cross the space's low ceiling. The radio is turned up loud and delivers the best music of the night from New York City's Hotel Roosevelt.

Each year another tenement neighbor hosts the year-end festivities. Each year, the basement is decorated the same. This year Concetta is the hostess. Aniella, Maddelana, and Giuseppina and their families, including grandchildren, ages 8 weeks to 18 years, arrive at the party at eight.

The children suffer the cheek-pinching ritual and the "Look-how-big-you-got" speech before they put on their party hats, grab old pots and lids to serve as noisemakers, and station themselves on the basement steps. With a bit of pushing and shoving, they line up and create a wall of people that is sure to endanger the descent of anyone older than forty. The babies are having the laughs of their lives as nonnas pass them from arm to arm.

The teen boys and girls eye one another. Most have not seen the others since a party on Memorial Day or Labor Day. Maddelana's son starts dancing the lindy with his daughter. That's enough of an invitation for others to start dancing. And her wise-guy teen grandson drags Concetta, the hostess, onto the floor and twirls her round and round. She giggles, blushes, and turns away quickly to get back to the stove and fry the zeppole, their traditional party treats.

The bowls of yeast-raised zeppole are on the table, along with a platter of American glazed ham, a huge casserole of gravy meat, and trays of as many pastas as there are Sundays. At least six other savory dishes with serving forks are on the long, portable buffet table. Drips of gravy from the meat have already made their way through the white paper tablecloth that proclaims "Happy New Year!"

But the zeppole are the stars of the show. They are swallowed up as quickly as they appear on the table. Some are dusted with powdered sugar. Others have bits of anchovy inside their airy centers.

The nonnas are fast friends; they have been for years—actually forever. But each nonna, licking the powdered sugar from her fingers or the salt of anchovies from her lips, has something to say about the zeppole.

"A little heavy," Maddelana says quietly.

"Too greasy," Giuseppina whispers.

"Not so-o-o bad," says Aniella, as she dusts her hands together.

In the meantime, they see no reason to walk away from the bowl Concetta regularly fills with new batches of golden brown puffs. They can never taste too many samples. Each compliments the cook, whose face is red and glistening from her stint dropping dough into boiling oil.

Still, Concetta also manages to zing the zeppole-making ability of one crony. She reminds them, "This year's zeppole are so much better than the ones we had last year." When she turns away, each finger-licking, lip-smacking nonna raises an eyebrow.

The moment is approaching when sentiment triumphs over snide asides. The children on the stairs begin to count down to midnight, imitating the voice of the radio announcer. A couple of teens have made it to the handholding stage. Husbands stand next to wives. Even grandfathers sidle up to grandmothers. It is the one time in the year when the grandchildren see their grandparents display affection toward each other.

"Five, four, three, two, one . . . Happy New Year!" And from the Hotel Roosevelt, Guy Lombardo and his Royal Canadians play "Auld Lang Syne." Every couple kisses; some dab at their eyes. The children bang pots and lids. The nonnas embrace. They do not mention the zeppole. They simply wish one another a healthy, happy New Year.

ZEPPOLE

Makes 18

1 package dry yeast
¼ teaspoon salt
2 teaspoons sugar
1 cup warm water
2 cups flour
3 cups light olive oil or corn oil
1 cup confectioners' sugar

Dissolve yeast and sugar in warm water; when yeast bubbles, add salt and flour; stir well.

Cover bowl tightly with plastic wrap; drape a kitchen towel over bowl.

Place bowl in a draft-free spot; allow dough to rise about 2 hours.

In a small Dutch oven or deep fryer, heat the oil to 375 degrees; oil should be at least 1 inch deep in the pan.

Use a tablespoon to drop dough into the hot oil; do not crowd.

Carefully drop the dough into the hot oil by heaping tablespoons.

Fry each portion of dough until golden brown on all sides.

Use a slotted spoon to remove from oil; place on paper towels to absorb any grease.

Sprinkle with confectioners' sugar; serve.

ZEPPOLE WITH ANCHOVIES
Separate a half portion of dough

Stir in 6 minced anchovies.

Fry as above in a separate pot or Dutch oven; serve immediately.

THANKS

Special thanks to my agent, Beth Davey, who worked tirelessly to find a home for the nonnas; to my designer, Noël Claro, for creating an elegant and beautiful book; to my photographer, Natasha Claro Southwick, for photos that are mouthwateringly inviting. Thanks to Carole Campana and Eileen Sansone for their exuberant cheerleading. Thank you: Chris, Karen, Danielle, Noël, Nicole, Fran Q, and Natasha for your invaluable suggestions and for blessing us with awe-inspiring grandchildren.

Thank you, Joe, for your patience and encouragement and for being a prince of a guy. There would be no story without you.

Fran Claro is a writer, editor, chef, baker and a long-time recipe archivist and creator. Her writing can be found in Scholastic Inc. publications, *The Dream Book: An Anthology of Writings by Italian American Women,* and on grandparents. com. She is nonna to 11 grandchildren; and lives in Westchester, NY, where she concocts Italian American feasts for her friends and family.

INDEX

A

Across the Alley (story), 31–32
Angeletti, 153
Anything for Thanksgiving?
    (story), 146–147

B

Baby Is Born, A (story), 179–180
Baccala Montecato, 180–181
Baccala. *See* Neapolitan Baccala;
    Sicilian Baccala.
Baked Pork and Beans, 91
Barley vs. Grain Spat, A (story),
    39–40
Beans. *See* Baked Pork and
    Beans; Escarole with Beans
    and "Bacon"; Romano Beans
    in Sauce; Romano Beans with
    Ham.
Beef Paprikash, 144–145
Biscotti, 156
Block Party, A (story), 85–87
Bread Salad, 13

C

Cake. *See* Coconut Jelly Layer
    Cake.
Calabrese Calamari, 176
Calamari. *See* Calabrese
    Calamari.
Caponata, 93–94
Celebrating a Saint (story),
    154–155

Chicken Milanese, 68–69
Chicken Scarpariello, 24
Chicken, Roast. *See* Roast
    Chicken.
Christmas Eve Feast, The (story),
    167–168
Church Ladies (story), 138–139
Coconut Jelly Layer Cake, 105
Cod puree. *See* Baccala
    Montecato.
Codfish in Tomato Sauce, 166
Cookies. *See* Angeletti; Regina
    Cookies.
Covering a Fig Tree (story),
    106–107
Cream, whipped Filling, 88
Cream Puffs, 87–88
Crostata Marmellata, 44–45

D

Dinner Party, A (story), 18–19
Dough, leftover, 45

E

Easter Grain Pie. *See* Pastiera.
Eggplant Parmigiana, 20–21
Eggplant Relish. *See* Caponata.
Eggs. *See* Onions and Eggs,
    Western omelet.
Eggs in Purgatory, 134
Escarole Pie. *See* Sicilian Escarole
    Pie.
Escarole with Beans and "Bacon",
    26–27

F

Fig Pizza, 107–108
Fire Hydrant Days (story), 67–68
Fireworks (story), 73–74
Fish. *See* Codfish in Tomato
  Sauce; Friday Night Fish
  Soup; Fritto Misto (Fried
  Fish); Neapolitan Baked Red
  Snapper; Neapolitan Fish
  Salad; Venetian Friday Fish.
Friday Night Fish Soup, 29–30
Frittata. *See* Potato Frittata.
Fritto Misto, 172–173

G

Getting Sauced (story), 58–59
Grain Pie. *See* Easter Grain Pie.
Granita. *See* Watermelon
  Granita.
Guarding the Fireside (story),
  89–90

H

Happy New Year (story), 182–184
Homework (story), 132–133
Hot Stuff (story), 95–96
How the Garden Grows (story),
  76–77
Hurry Up . . . The Bride's Getting
  Out of the Car (story), 10–12

I

"Instant" Gravy and Meatballs,
  59–61
In the Style of the Shoemaker
  (story), 22–23
It's All in a Name (story), 55–56

J

Jam Tart. *See* Crostata
  Marmellata.
Jelly layer cake. *See* Coconut Jelly
  Layer Cake.

L

Lasagna Genovese, 127–128
Layer cake. *See* Coconut Jelly
  Layer Cake.
Lemon-Iced Cookies. *See*
  Angeletti.
Let the Season Start (story),
  150–152
Live Show, A (story), 46–47
Livornese Pasta with Clam Sauce,
  175

M

Macaroni and Gravy, 118–120
Macaroni's in the Basement—
  The Wake Is Upstairs, the
  (story), 117–118
Meatballs. *See* "Instant" Gravy
  and Meatballs.
Mushrooms. *See* Stuffed
  Mushrooms.
Mussels. *See* Sicilian Mussels
My Town's Better Than Your
  Town (story), 92–93

N

Name Game, The (story), 82–83
Neapolitan Baccala, 171
Neapolitan Baked Red Snapper,
  174–175
Neapolitan Fish Salad, 173

Neapolitan Pasta, 170
Neapolitan Spinach Pie, 178
New Spot for a Garden (story), 43–44
Nonnas and the Red Menace (story), 161–162

O

Olive Salad, 17
Omelet. *See* Western Omelet.
Onions and Eggs, 123

P

Palm Sunday (story), 34–36
Pasta. *See* Livornese Pasta with Clam Sauce; Neapolitan Pasta; Pasta with Anchovies; Pasta with Peas and Pancetta; Sicilian Pasta with Sardines.
Pasta with Anchovies, 163
Pasta with Peas and Pancetta, 111–112
Pastiera, 41–42
Peaches in Red Wine, 101
Pears Simmered in Red Wine, 102
Peppers. *See* Sausage and Peppers; Slow-Fried Hot Peppers.
Photographic Memories (story), 126–127
Pie. *See* Easter Grain Pie; Neapolitan Spinach Pie; Sicilian Escarole Pie.
Piecework (story), 129–130
Pizza Rustica, 37–38
Pizza. *See* Fig Pizza; Pizza Rustica.

Popcorn, 115
Porchetta, 53–54
Pork and Beans, Baked, 91
Pork Chops with Wine and Sage, 33
Pork Roast. *See* Porchetta.
Pot Roast. *See* Stuffato.
Potato Frittata, 72
Preserving the Past (story), 103–104
Price Wars (story), 25–26
Problems! Problems! (story), 110–111

Q

Queen of the Transfers (story), 164–165

R

Ready for a Wedding (story), 157–158
Regina Cookies, 137
Ribollita, 140–141
Ricotta Cream Filling, 88
Roast Chicken, 47–48
Romano Beans in Sauce, 83–84
Romano Beans with Ham, 84

S

Saint's Big Day, The (story), 52–53
Salad, 69. *See also* Bread Salad; Olive Salad.
Sand in Their Shoes (story), 70–71
Saturday at the Movies (story), 49–50
Sausage and Peppers, 12–13

Semi-Private Bath, A (story), 28–29
Sewing for Fun (story), 135–136
Sicilian Baccala, 172
Sicilian Escarole Pie, 177
Sicilian Mussels, 173–174
Sicilian Pasta with Sardines, 169
Slow-Fried Hot Peppers, 97
Snapper. *See* Neapolitan Baked Red Snapper.
Soup. *See* Ribollita; Wedding Soup.
Spiedini, 131
Spinach Pie. *See* Neapolitan Spinach Pie.
Statue's Eyes Moved—Really, The (story), 124–125
Steak Pizzaiola, 51
Storefront Caravan, A (story), 142–143
Stuffato, 57
Stuffed Mushrooms, 148
Stuffed Zucchini Blossoms, 80–81
Stuffed Zucchini, 77–78

T
Taralli, 115
Toss Me a Salami: The Football Wedding (story), 14–16

TV Time (story), 113–115

V
Veal Parmigiana, 75
Venetian Friday Fish, 125

W
War of the Flowers, The (story), 79–80
Watermelon Granita, 65–66
Waw-dee-mell-OWN, Tutti Frutti, and the Ladies from the Block (story), 63–65
We Need the Eggs (story), 98–99
Wedding Soup, 158–160
Western Omelet, 99
Winery—in Brooklyn? (story), 100–101
World at Their Doorstep, The (story), 121–123

Z
Zeppole, 184–185
    with Anchovies, 185
Zucchini Blossom Frittata, 81
Zucchini Blossoms, Stuffed, 80–81
Zucchini. *See* Stuffed Zucchini.